Freedom, Loyalty, Dissent

MENO: *I feel, somehow, that I like what you are saying.*

SOCRATES: *And I, Meno, like what I am saying. Some things I have said of which I am not altogether confident. But that we shall be better and braver and less helpless if we think that we ought to enquire, than we should have been if we indulged in the idle fancy that there was no knowing and no use in seeking to know what we do not know; — that is a theme upon which I am ready to fight, in word and deed, to the utmost of my power.*

FREEDOM
LOYALTY
DISSENT

By HENRY STEELE COMMAGER

New York • OXFORD UNIVERSITY PRESS • 1954

To Steele

Preface

THE ESSAYS now collected in this volume were written at different times and for different occasions over a period of six years, but all are bound together by a common theme and a unified point of view. The theme, alas more relevant today than it was even in 1947, when the first of these essays was written, is the necessity of freedom in a society such as the American; the point of view is practical and pragmatic. The argument that runs through all of these papers is that we must preserve and encourage the exercise of freedom of inquiry, investigation, dissent, association, education, science, literature, politics—freedom, in short, in all of its manifestations, not as an abstract right but as an imperative necessity. Freedom is not a luxury that we can indulge in when at last we have security and prosperity and enlightenment; it is, rather, antecedent to all of these, for without it we can have neither security nor prosperity nor enlightenment.

'Who Is Loyal to America?' appeared first in *Harper's Magazine*; 'Free Enterprise in Ideas' in the *Saturday Review*; 'Guilt by Association?' in much abbreviated form in *The New York Times Magazine.* 'The Necessity of Freedom' was given, in somewhat different form, as one of the Cooper Foundation lectures at Swarthmore College, and 'The Necessity of Experimentation' as one of the Telluride lectures at Cornell University. I am grateful to the editors of these magazines and the sponsors of these lectureships for permission to revise and reprint these papers here.

Henry Steele Commager

February 1954

Contents

Freedom, Loyalty, Dissent

I

The Necessity of Freedom

FREEDOM OF SPEECH and of the press — that is, freedom of inquiry, criticism, and dissent — are guaranteed in state and federal constitutions now over a century and a half old. It is a sobering fact, however, that each generation has to vindicate these freedoms anew, and for itself. Yet this is not wholly a misfortune; one might almost see in it Providential wisdom. For there are risks in taking things for granted, risks not only of failure to appreciate them but of failure to understand them. Freedoms vindicated anew are more precious than those achieved without effort, and only those who are required to justify freedom can fully understand it.

Certainly the responsibility of vindicating the claims of freedom confronts us now in urgent fashion. There have been previous examples of a challenge to freedom in our own history — the

3

so-called Red hysteria of the early nineteen-
twenties comes to mind — but we have to go back
to the history of the ante-bellum South for anything comparable in scale or character to what
we are witnessing today: a broad official and non-
official attack upon nonconformity. It is unnecessary to describe this attack; its manifestations are, alas, familiar enough. It is with the
deeper implications and the far-reaching consequences of the attack on freedom that we are
concerned here, and with the problem of preserv-
ing freedom in a society wracked by fear and
confused by counsels of unreason.

How are we to vindicate the claims of freedom?
More specifically, how are we to vindicate the
claims of criticism and dissent and nonconformity? There are various ways we might go about
such a vindication, some more familiar, some perhaps more persuasive, than others. There is, for
example, the constitutional or legal approach to
the whole question. We could submit the Bills
of Rights, state and federal; recall the long and
glorious history of these parts of our Constitutions; cite relevant court decisions — among them
some of the most eloquent and moving documents in our literature. A persuasive, even a con-

clusive, constitutional case could be made out against some of the practices of state and Congressional Un-American Activities Committees, or against such acts as the McCarran Internal Security Bill.

Or there is what we may call the natural rights approach, an approach which could be launched with equal effect from experience or from theory. This approach emphasizes what was once familiar enough to all Americans — and what we are now in danger of forgetting — that government derives its powers from men; that rights of life and liberty are inalienable; that these rights are not something that government graciously confers upon men, but things no government can take away from men. This approach is profoundly concerned with Right — usually with individual Right.

This is another way of saying that it is concerned with what must deeply concern all of us — the dignity of man. It is from this basic philosophical principle that the natural rights argument derives much of its strength. For it is becoming increasingly clear that it is respect for the dignity of the individual that most sharply differentiates democratic from totalitarian systems. Granted this basic principle, it follows that any conduct of the state that impairs the dignity of man is dangerous. And any argument for conformity that finds its ultimate sanction in force rather than in reason strikes at the integrity of the individual, and thus at the basic principle of democracy.

But it must be confessed that neither the legalistic nor the natural rights approach to this problem of freedom is wholly satisfactory. The legal issue is almost always a bit obscure; after all, neither the Alien and Sedition Acts of the 1790's nor the Sedition and Espionage Acts of the First World War were held void by the courts, while the Smith Act of 1940 has so far been sustained. And we must, in all fairness, go even further than this. Those who have concern for the preservation of elementary freedoms must not take refuge in legalism. It is not sufficient for freedom to be vindicated by the courts, or by constitutional experts. That is, in a sense, a barren vindication. If the preservation of our freedom depends upon the courts then we are, indeed, lost, for in the long run neither courts nor Constitution can save us from our own errors, follies, or wickedness.

Nor, for all its persuasiveness and its deep moral appeal, is the argument from natural rights conclusive. After all, it will be said, there are no rights outside society. After all, at a time of mortal danger, we cannot be too sensitive about individual rights or individual dignity — we who so readily grant the state the right to exact life and limb from our young men. After all, it will be argued, if our society and our government go under, all philosophical notions of natural rights or the dignity of the individual will be of antiquarian interest merely. Or — it will be added — concern for rights in the abstract is a sentimental luxury. 'There is no right to be wrong,' the Irish statesman De Valera has said, and in one form or another that attitude is widespread. Up to a certain point, so the argument runs, we can tolerate with good humor those who deny the axioms of Euclid, and we can tolerate them because they are harmless. But we do not allow them to teach mathematics. Nor do we, for example, tolerate on the highways those who insist that red is green or green is red; we take their licenses away from them.

We need not subscribe wholly to any of these objections to admit that they contain some elements of truth and of plausibility. The case for freedom — especially the case for freedom of dissent and for heterodoxy — rests not only on the familiar and fundamental arguments of constitutional right and natural rights, but on one other that is equally persuasive, and that seems to me conclusive. That is the argument of the pragmatic necessity for freedom.

* * * *

Logically there might seem to be a deep gap between natural rights and pragmatism. The natural rights argument is transcendental; the pragmatic argument is experimental. Transcendentalism is the philosophy of absolutes; pragmatism says damn the absolute. Transcendentalism is inspired by truths that transcend proof; pragmatism will have no commerce with notions until they have submitted themselves to proof. The natural rights approach to the problem of freedom, then, establishes the principles that freedom is an absolute right and that it is an absolute good, and with these principles most of us would agree. Yet the principles are flouted or repudiated, and we must confess that they are either too complex to be understood or too weak to be effective, or perhaps that we are so lacking in virtue that we are not prepared to accept in practice those truths we acknowledge in principle. The pragmatic approach is a different one. It asks first the familiar question: What are the practical consequences of a course of conduct which denies or fetters freedom? It is when we ask this question, consider its implications, and work out an answer that it becomes clear that freedom is not only a right but a necessity.

Happily these two approaches to our problem, the ideal and the practical, are not mutually exclusive. In defiance of logic, but in response to powerful instincts, Americans have always been both transcendental and pragmatic. They have used both philosophies — used them, sometimes, interchangeably. You will find them in the first great document of our national history, the Declaration of Independence. 'We hold these truths to be self-evident,' wrote Jefferson, and there spoke the transcendentalist; 'that whenever government becomes destructive of these ends' — there spoke the pragmatist. The alliance of transcendentalist and pragmatist persisted through the nineteenth century, in the North. The New England reformers were, most of them, transcendentalists, but it is relevant to notice that they did not act like the idealists and transcendentalists of Germany and France and England. They acted, rather, like the utilitarians of England. They Americanized transcendentalism, put it to work, made it justify itself pragmatically. They not only insisted upon inalienable rights, but looked to the consequences of the denial of those rights — the consequences to freedom, to democracy, to the minds and souls of men. That is a large part of the meaning of the generation of 1830 to 1860 — the generation of Channing and Parker, Emerson and Thoreau, Horace Mann and Margaret Fuller, Garrison and Howe and Phillips, and the others whose names still blaze like battle flags.

Nor did the pragmatists, in turn, wholly abandon transcendentalism; rather they built upon it. William James's war was not with the transcendentalists, many of whom he had loved and honored in his youth; it was with the Hegelians. Though he wanted to put every notion to the test of experience, he himself did not abandon those affluent assumptions that had so long sustained his society — assumptions about the essential virtue of man, the superiority of truth over error, of freedom over slavery.

There is, then, nothing inharmonious about combining the idealistic and the pragmatic attitudes toward the problem of freedom in our time. Nor can we, alas, assume that these two philosophical approaches to the problem are so familiar and instinctive that they need not be invoked. Past generations have preferred one or the other of these two philosophical attitudes; it has remained for ours to pay lip-service to both, and to ignore both. Uncertain of principles, we fall back on emotion; unfamiliar with the past, we are afraid of the future. Increasingly we look to men, ideas, and institutions not from the point of view of how they work, but from the point of view of how they ought to work if they conformed to our *a priori* ideas about them: we are like the Italian woman William James describes, who sat on the sidewalk in New York handing out cards which said that she had come to America to raise money to enable her to return to Italy! Increasingly we set up abstract standards, and then require that men and institutions conform to them. Thus we judge enterprise not by the energies it releases or the ends it achieves, but by its supposed conformity to the shibboleths of Herbert Spencer. Thus we judge colleges and universities not by their actual character or their accomplishments, but by the alleged views of their members on subjects we choose to regard as crucial. Thus we judge organizations not by what they do, but by the supposed views of their members. Thus we judge the validity of the popular election of the President not by the way it has actually operated over a century and a half but by how it might operate if majorities whose judgment we fear continue their habit of voting for the men they want; and we write into the Constitution — where it does not belong — a limitation on the exercise of the majority will in this decisive arena. Thus we judge foreign policy not by the realities of international relations, but by the extent to which these realities conform to our preconceptions of what they ought to be. Thus we judge loyalty not by conduct but by gestures and ceremonies. Our political and constitutional processes are coming to be a vulgar competition in eloquence about loyalty and rhetoric about patriotism.

But let us turn without more ado to the pragmatic necessity for freedom. What is the argument here? It is the argument of consequences. 'The pragmatic method,' William James wrote, 'starts from the postulate that there is no difference of truth that doesn't make a difference of fact somewhere, and it seeks to determine the meaning of all differences of opinion by making the discussion hinge as soon as possible upon some practical or particular issue.'

What, then, are the practical consequences of the attack upon independence of thought, non-conformity, dissent, which is now gathering momentum everywhere in the land? What kind of society will it create? What climate of opinion will it encourage? What will be its effect on science and scholarship, on politics and diplomacy, on security and peace? What, in short, is happening to us and what is likely to happen to us if we persist in penalizing dissent and rewarding orthodoxy?

The first and most obvious consequence is that we shall arrive, sooner or later, at an official standard of orthodoxy or — to use the current term — loyalty. It is, to be sure, one of the more curious features of the current drive against disloyalty and subversion that we so far lack definitions of either term.[1] Yet definitions are in

---

[1] The Constitution, to be sure, carefully defines treason, but this definition is customarily ignored or flouted by the professional guardians of the Constitution!

the making — in the making not so much by
Congress or the courts, as in the minds of millions of Americans, in the daily press, in the
schoolroom, in magazines and books, pulpits and
forums, and a thousand other vehicles and channels of opinion. If you are going to penalize
disloyalty, you must first determine what loyalty
is; if you are going to silence nonconformity, you
must determine what conformity is — and to
what it conforms. If you are going to accept
J. Edgar Hoover's 'easy test' of an organization:
'Does it have a consistent record of support to the
American viewpoint?' — you must determine
what is the American viewpoint. If you are going
to dismiss men from office or from teaching posts
for membership in subversive organizations, you
must eventually draw up a list not only of those
that are subversive but of those that are patriotic.
If you are going to silence dangerous ideas you
must establish what ideas are safe.

To whom shall we entrust these great and
delicate tasks? This is not a rhetorical question;
it is an urgently practical one. Who, in our government or our society, is to determine what
ideas are safe?

We need not conjure up, here, an organization

like the 'Thought Police,' or a set of crimes like 'Crime Think,' of George Orwell's *1984*. It is not necessary to resort to that. The most effective censorship is not, in fact, legal; in a democracy — as Tocqueville pointed out in *Democracy in America* — it is public opinion. The danger is not that laws may, in the end, cut us off from that body of independent and original thought that we so urgently need; it is rather that public opinion may create a situation where independence and originality simply do not emerge. That is even more serious. The greatest danger that threatens us is neither heterodox thought nor orthodox thought, but the absence of thought.

The second consequence of penalizing non-conformity, originality, and independence is a very practical one, and it is one whose effects are already being felt in many quarters. It is simply this: first-rate men and women will not and cannot work under conditions fixed by those who are afraid of ideas. Scholars who have to run the gauntlet of legislative investigations of their teaching, their writing, their associations, will look elsewhere for work — or will turn to purely antiquarian research. Scientists who cannot exchange information because of the requirements

of security will fail to get essential information —
or will refuse to work under conditions that all
but guarantee ineffective and inconclusive work.
Civil servants, or potential government employees, faced with one investigation after another,
with the overshadowing danger of smears from
House or from Senate, with harassment and
suspicion, will prefer employment in private
industry.

It will be useful to determine, a generation
from now, whether those universities that have
purged their faculties are actually stronger than
they were before the purges occurred — stronger
in those essentials that go to make a university.
It will be valuable to discover whether the civil
service is, in fact, more loyal — with all the implications of that tremendous word — than the old
civil service of the pre-loyalty investigation years.
It will be important to know whether science
advances as rapidly under the protection of security as it advanced before the days of elaborate
security regulations or whether it makes greater
progress in the United States than in England,
where security arrangements are eminently mod-
erate and sensible and are administered with a
nice regard for individual rights.

A third consequence of the demand for conformity grows out of the first two. It is the development in this country of the kind of society in which freedom of inquiry does not flourish, in which criticism does not flourish, in which originality does not flourish. This is no alarmist bugaboo; it is a development already under way. Already civil servants are afraid to read certain magazines or to join certain organizations. Already teachers hesitate to discuss certain issues in class; not long ago the New York City Board of Education sought to reassure them on this: you may discuss communism objectively, it said, as long as you tell pupils how wicked it all is! Already men and women hesitate to join minority parties or 'dangerous' organizations, or to agitate for reform. And well they might! Some time ago a much decorated Negro army captain was asked to resign from the service because he was charged with reading the *Daily Worker* and because his father was alleged to have fought segregation in public housing. The demand was, to be sure, withdrawn. But how many instances of such official stupidity go undiscovered, unpublicized, and unchallenged? [2] How many soldiers,

---

[2] These absurdities continue. Thus in the fall of 1953 First Lieutenant J. Radulovich, then studying at the Uni-

duly impressed by the risks involved, were dis-
suaded by this episode from reading anything
but the comics? Do we want the kind of army
that will read only approved literature?

It is, you see, with the practical consequences
to our society of the limitations on freedom that
we are concerned. We do not protect freedom in
order to indulge error. We protect freedom in
order to discover truth. We do not maintain
freedom in order to permit eccentricity to flourish; we maintain freedom in order that society
may profit from criticism, even eccentric criticism. We do not encourage dissent for sentimental reasons; we encourage dissent because we
cannot live without it.

versity of Michigan, was dropped by the Air Force because
of his 'close continuous association' with two dubious
characters — his father, who was alleged to read pro-Communist publications, and his sister, who allegedly had displayed Communist sympathies. There were no charges
against Lieutenant Radulovich himself. Questioned on
this act, Secretary of Defense Wilson said that in the
event of a conflict between the interests of an individual
and the interests of the nation, the individual interest
had to give way; it did not apparently occur to him that
it was to the interest of the nation to see that justice was
done a member of the armed services. Secretary Talbott
ultimately overruled the recommendation of the Air
Force colonels and retained Lieutenant Radulovich in the
Reserve.

Let us turn, for our illustrations, from the general to the particular. The House Un-American Activities Committee has launched an attack on the Lawyers' Guild as a pro-Communist or 'subversive' organization.[3] The chief basis for this attack is, as far as we know, that the Guild has proffered its services to the defense of Communists under indictment for violation of the Smith Act. We need not inquire here into the accuracy of this charge or into the degree of zeal displayed by the Lawyers' Guild. Let us ask rather what are the logical conclusions to be drawn by the position which the House Committee has adopted? They are two: that certain criminals are so despicable that they are not entitled to counsel, and that a lawyer who defends a criminal is himself sympathetic to crime. If these principles are once officially established, what happens to the Anglo-American principle that everyone, even the worst criminal, has a right to his day in court? This principle was established not out of sentimental sympathy for criminals; it was established because it was the only way of insuring that justice would be done.

[3] This attack has now (1954) been given a semi-official character by the Attorney General.

If this principle goes by the board, under pressure from communism, then communism has won a notable victory; it has overturned our century-old devotion to the doctrine of due process of law.[4]

Here is a second illustration. Some time ago a Jersey City junior college removed from its li-

[4] Note that the Canon of Legal Ethics provides (Canon 15) that a lawyer owes 'entire devotion to the interests of the client. . . No fear of judicial disfavor or public unpopularity should restrain him from the full discharge of his duty.' A Report of a Special Committee of the American Bar Association of July 1953 states that 'American lawyers generally recognize that it is the duty of the Bar to see that all defendants, however unpopular, have the benefit of counsel for their defense.' Yet persons charged with subversive activities are finding it almost impossible to obtain counsel. In the Baltimore case of *U. S.* v. *Frankfeld* defendants appealed in vain to more than thirty lawyers to take their case. In the case of *Commonwealth of Pennsylvania* v. *Nelson* the defendant was forced to represent himself in a trial for sedition after having appealed in vain to 700 lawyers in Pittsburgh and other Eastern cities. In the case of *U. S.* v. *Flynn et al.,* defendants submitted to the U.S. Circuit Court of Appeals an affidavit stating that 'they have written to more than twenty-eight law firms throughout the country requesting an interview to discuss the retainer of said firms on the appeal therein. Of this number twelve did not reply at all to appellants' requests; and all sixteen who did reply refused to grant the requested interview on the grounds that they either could not or would not accept a retainer herein.'

brary shelves all works written by or edited by
Mark Van Doren. The charge against this distinguished poet and critic was that he had associated
with the wrong people; the taint of that association infected, it would seem, not only Mr. Van
Doren's poetry and criticism, but his editions of
Shakespeare, Milton, and Wordsworth as well.[5]
What happened to Mr. Van Doren's books is
symptomatic. Censorship of textbooks is flourishing throughout the country, though it rarely
reaches the dizzy heights of imbecility attained
by the Jersey City junior college.[6] Everywhere
textbooks of history, politics, and economics are
under attack by patriotic or filiopietistic organizations such as the American Legion or the Daughters of the American Revolution, by economic
organizations like the National Association of
Manufacturers and the Chambers of Commerce,
or by liberal organizations like the National
Association for the Advancement of Colored
People. Whatever the animus of the attack, the
principle is the same. It is the principle of censor-

[5] The books were subsequently restored to their shelves.
[6] Some communities in Texas, however, would go even
further and remove, or stigmatize by special label, books
merely *illustrated* by someone named in a list of 'subversives.'

ship. It is the principle of conformity. It is the principle which assumes that truth is known, and that anything that deviates from this known truth — known to the members of the particular organization — is heresy.

Now we cannot but be indignant when injustice is done a scholar like Mr. Van Doren, and it is right that we should be indignant. Yet it is not the effect of censorship on the author or, for that matter, on the publisher, that is significant. What is significant is the effect of such censorship on our educational system — on boards of education, on superintendents, on teachers, on the boys and girls, the young men and young women, who are the end-product of the whole thing. For if you succeed in banning or censoring textbooks written by men who are critical and independent, you will get textbooks written by men who are not critical or independent, or by men who, given a choice between intellectual independence and sales, settle for the sales. If you penalize publishers for publishing textbooks by scholars who are critical, you will speedily enough persuade them to publish textbooks by writers — I do not say scholars — who are not critical. If you punish teachers for using books that organized patriots or conservatives or radicals happen to disapprove, you will get, eventually, the kind of teacher who uses the book he is told to use by the most vociferous organization. These are the people who will, in the end, direct the education of our children: writers who express no ideas because all ideas are dangerous or expensive; boards of education that are timid; teachers who are willing to conform. What kind of teaching are we going to have? What kind of students are we going to turn out? Are we, by this method, going to train a generation of students competent to deal with the difficult and complex problems of the modern world?

We may take a third example from the same arena — that of education. Let us contemplate, for a moment, the efforts of boards of regents and alumni associations and others to protect students in colleges and universities from dangerous ideas. This, too, is a nation-wide phenomenon, found alike at Harvard and at California, in Texas and in Michigan. We have one rather elaborate case study of this demand for conformity: the University of California.[7] Let

[7] See George R. Stewart, *The Year of the Oath* (1950).

us look at the consequences, to that institution and to that state, of the drive for conformity.

Notice, first, that we use the term 'conformity.' The ostensible reason for the requirement of special loyalty oaths at California was fear of communism, but that was quickly abandoned. The most elaborate investigation did not discover any Communists on any of the faculties of the University, yet the trustees did not abandon their demand in the face of this evidence, but persisted in it as a test of authority. The real issue — here as in Texas and elsewhere — was not communism but 'dangerous thoughts.' A prominent member of the Board of Regents, Charles C. Teague, put the matter succinctly in a letter to President Sproul:

'I have a profound conviction that freedom in the world is being destroyed by Communism, of which Socialism is the first step. Freedom has been destroyed in England by Socialism, and the United States has travelled a considerable distance along the same line. It has been demonstrated many times that Socialism destroys incentive and reduces production.'

What is most interesting here is that a member of the Board of Regents should tell the President —

and through him the faculty — what is 'demonstrated' truth, and that he should assume that his
own 'profound convictions' are identical with cosmic laws. Clearly, if he is right, anyone who
departs from his position is guilty of error —
which is to say, of heresy. But if he already knows
demonstrated truth in the field of economics and
of politics, then the departments of economics
and politics at the University are superfluous.
The philosophy of Mr. Teague's argument does
not differ in any essentials from the philosophy
behind Nazi and Communist control of university teaching.[8]

What have been the consequences of the demand for conformity from the Regents of the
University of California? It has not rid the

[8] The Supreme Court of California decided, in 1951,
that the requirement of a loyalty oath was unconstitutional. Speaking for a unanimous Court, Judge Peek held
that 'if the faculty of the University can be subjected to
any more narrow test of loyalty than the constitutional
oath, the constitutional mandate . . . would be effectively
frustrated, and our great institution now dedicated to
learning and the search for truth reduced to an organ
for the propagation of the ephemeral political, religious,
social and economic philosophies, whatever they may be,
of the majority of the Board of Regents of that moment.'
Thus in the end it was Mr. Teague and his Board who
were revealed as the true subversives.

faculty of Communists, because there were no Communists. It has, however — and here we quote an investigation by the California Civil Liberties Union —

'cost a year of horror and failure for students, teachers, and administrations; the firing of twenty-six instructors; the dropping of forty or fifty regular courses; the resignation of a large number of professors; the refusal of many well-known scholars to accept appointment; condemnation of the Regents' action by faculties of other universities and learned societies; and a general loss of confidence in the University. . . In the long record of higher education no offense against freedom and justice has equalled in scope the ruthlessness of the offense now committed at the University.'

What was gained, and what was lost? Clearly nothing was gained. But what price have the Regents paid for the luxury of their grandstand gesture against the Kremlin? The Kremlin, it may be assumed, is not seriously shaken; indeed, it must rejoice at this flattery by imitation. The important question is, what price has been paid by the scholars, the scientists, the students of the present and of the future?

On this whole matter of the teaching of 'dangerous ideas' there is one observation that might well be carved in the meeting room of the Board of Regents and Trustees of every college and university. It is an observation by Whitelaw Reid, one-time owner and editor of the *New York Tribune,* and it was made in 1873:

'As for the scholar, the laws of his intellectual development may be trusted to fix his place. Free thought is necessarily aggressive and critical. The scholar, like the healthy, red-blooded young man, is an inherent, an organic, an inevitable radical. It is his business to reverse the epigram of Emerson, and put the best men and the best cause together. And so, we may set down, as a . . . function of the American scholar in politics, an intellectual leadership of the radicals.'

Let us turn to a fourth illustration of the attack upon independence and nonconformity: Senator McCarthy's assault upon the State Department and particularly upon Professor Lattimore and other Far Eastern experts. The Tydings Committee called Senator McCarthy's charges 'a fraud and a hoax perpetrated on the Senate of the United States and the American people,' but their significance goes much further than this. For we must ponder thoughtfully the consequences of McCarthy's attack, and of that

entire body of irresponsible criticism which finds
its inspiration in the success of the Senator from
Wisconsin. One consequence is that the assailants
have partly succeeded in denying to the State Department the confidence of the American people.
Another is that American prestige abroad has
suffered serious impairment. A third is that the
Department is far less able to concentrate on the
central task of conducting foreign relations, but
must dissipate its energies on the marginal tasks
of defending itself and its staff against whatever
charges any Congressman may choose to bring
up, for whatever reasons. A fourth is that the
Department is finding it increasingly difficult to
recruit first-rate men for the important jobs it
has to do.[9] A fifth is that Department officials

[9] In *Fire in the Ashes,* Theodore White has an interesting chapter on the impact of McCarthyism on our
Foreign Service, especially on the China Service. 'The
basic burden of the reporting of the China Service in the
critical years was that, in the inevitable clash between the
Chinese Communists and Chiang Kai-shek, Chiang would
be the loser. This correctness in judgment has resulted,
however, not in honor either collectively or individually
to the China Service. China has gone Communist. In
some fashion the men of the China Service were held
responsible. The China Service, therefore, no longer exists. Of the 22 officers who joined it before the beginning
of World War II, there were in 1952 only two still used
by the State Department in Washington. . . Most of the

fearful of eventual investigations, are hesitant about speaking their minds, reporting all the facts that come to them.[10] Who knows, after all, what some future McCarthy may not do with such reports? A sixth is that hereafter experts will think twice before giving advice to the State Department and that the Department will think twice before calling in the experts. For the McCarthy charges and their aftermath establish this principle: it is dangerous to give disinterested advice if anyone in Congress — or perhaps on the radio — disapproves of the advice you

rest were still serving the American government, but not in Formosa, Japan, Central Intelligence or anywhere else where their intimate knowledge of a China with whom we were desperately at war in Korea might be useful' (pp. 376-7).

[10] In a letter to *The New York Times* of 17 January 1954, five veteran diplomats, Norman Armour, Robert Woods Bliss, Joseph C. Grew, William Phillips, and G. Howland Shaw, write: 'Recently the Foreign Service has been subjected to a series of attacks from outside sources which have questioned the loyalty and the moral standards of its members. With rare exceptions the justification for these attacks has been so flimsy as to have no standing in a court of law or in the mind of any individual capable of differentiating repeated accusation from even a reasonable presumption of guilt. Nevertheless these attacks have had sinister results.

'The conclusion has become inescapable, for instance, that a Foreign Service officer who reports on persons and

give. It is as if we should call in five or six
doctors to diagnose an ailment, get a diagnosis of
cancer, and then denounce the doctors as traitors
to their oath, charlatans and marplots, and try
to get them excluded from practice. If we were
powerful enough we might be successful, but we
would find some difficulty in getting a doctor
next time we were sick.

By denouncing as Communists or traitors
those who gave us unpalatable advice, we have
in a sense cut ourselves off from unpalatable
advice. But that is the kind we need — almost
the only kind we need; the other kind we can
work up for ourselves. And the moral here is
plain. If we penalize critics we shall cut our-

events to the very best of his ability and who makes
recommendations which at the time he conscientiously
believes to be in the interest of the United States may
subsequently find his loyalty and integrity challenged
and may even be forced out of the service and discredited
forever as a private citizen after many years of distinguished service. A premium therefore has been put upon
reporting and upon recommendations which are ambigu-
ously stated or so cautiously set forth as to be deceiving.

'When any such tendency begins its insidious work it
is not long before accuracy and initiative have been sacri-
ficed to acceptability and conformity. The ultimate result
is a threat to national security. In this connection the
history of the Nazi and Fascist foreign services before the
Second World War is pertinent.'

selves off from criticism. If we cut ourselves off from criticism we are likely to make mistakes. If we wish to avoid mistakes, we must create an atmosphere that encourages criticism.

It is not as if we were without experience with nations that had adopted the policy of official conformity, or with the contest between the forces of freedom and those of fear. After all, it is no accident that the nations dedicated to freedom won the two great wars of the twentieth century, and those committed to totalitarianism went under. And the more we learn about the inner history of Germany and Japan during the Second World War, the clearer it becomes that the seeds of their defeat were planted in the systems to which they were dedicated — in the suppression of criticism and dissent and the insistence upon acquiescence and conformity. Nor need we go to the Old World or to the Orient for examples; we have had experience even in our own history, and that experience is illuminating.

From about 1830 to the Civil War, the South was committed to a position in economics, sociology, politics, and philosophy, that was all but impervious to criticism. This was the view that

slavery was a positive good and that it was the
cornerstone of a prosperous South. In defense of
this peculiar institution, the South drove out,
silenced, or suppressed her critics. In defense of
this institution, otherwise virtuous and intelligent gentlemen burned books, banned mail, got
rid of preachers who preached the wrong doctrines and of editors who wrote the wrong senti-
ments, purged the schools and the colleges of
dissenters. They were sure that they knew truth,
and that all who disagreed with them or who
criticized them were not only wrong but subversive. And — in part because they closed their
ears to criticism and dissent — they led their section down the road to war and to ruin.

*　*　*　*

We have been very busy, of late, calculating
our resources and the resources of our potential
enemies — and that calculation is going on all
over the globe. The calculation is customarily
made in terms of wealth, resources, manpower,
military leadership, atomic and other weapons,
allies and associates, and so forth — that is, it is
customarily made in material terms.

For whatever may be the balance on military

resources — the atomic weapon versus manpower, logistical superiority versus air power, and so forth — there is one realm where our superiority is beyond challenge, and where it cannot be lost except by our own will. Ours is a system of freedom — freedom of inquiry, of investigation, of criticism, and of creation. Our science is unfettered. Our inventiveness is untrammeled. Our ability to inquire and criticize and resolve is unlimited. Ours is, in short, an open system, with limitless possibilities for improvement. Over against it stands the closed system of totalitarian countries. In this system, facts have to conform to preconceived ideas, or so much the worse for the facts. If biology does not justify Marx and Lenin, then you get a new biology. If music does not harmonize with Communist ideas, you reform or purge your musicians. If history does not exalt communism, you rewrite history. And if politics and diplomacy abroad do not fit into your preconceived framework, then you regard them as fraudulent and cherish your framework. This demand that facts conform to ideas extends to the whole world of affairs — to the military, the political, and the economic, as well as the cultural. Thus the Communists are the prisoners of their own system. They cannot adjust their conduct to reality for they recognize only those realities that flatter their preconceptions. They cannot profit by experience, for they accept only the experience that fits the pattern of their ideas. They cannot learn through criticism, for they do not allow criticism.

Ours is a different philosophy, a different tradition, and a different and happier prospect. Because we are free we can, if we will, avoid errors. We can experiment. We can criticize. We can adjust and accommodate and compromise. We can air our grievances and remedy them. Our scientists can follow where science leads. Our historians and economists can follow the track of truth. We are not committed to our mistakes. We are not committed to irretrievable errors or irreversible policies. We do not — so far — require that all those who are with us agree on everything, subscribe to a formula, follow a pattern. But we are in danger of doing just that and of forfeiting what is, in the last analysis, our greatest advantage. By insisting upon conformity in the intellectual arena and by threatening with disapproval all those who dissent or who give us unpopular advice, we are in danger of following

the totalitarian philosophy — and the totalitarian
mistakes.

It would be absurd to say that only a society
dedicated to freedom can win victories. Soviet
Russia is not dedicated to freedom, and she has
won a good many victories. But the most impres-
sive thing about Russia in her relations with the
non-Communist world is that she has made
calamitous mistakes and suffered serious defeats.
She made a mistake at Potsdam in demanding
too much for Poland, and thus setting the stage
for future suspicion. She made a mistake in her
treatment of Yugoslavia and forfeited that alliance. She made mistakes in her relations with
Turkey to the south and Finland to the north,
and can count on hostility in those places rather
than friendship. She made a mistake in failing
to join the Marshall Plan. She made a major
mistake in forcing the Western nations together
in a European Defense community, thus raising
up formidable power against her. She made —
and is continuing to make — mistakes in her
atomic policies. The uprisings in eastern Germany suggest that she is making irretrievable
mistakes in her government of occupied and
satellite territories. Many if not all of these mis-

takes are mistakes of judgment — that is, they are
traceable to the failure to be well informed and
to encourage or even permit criticism and dissent.

It is correct to say that a people like ourselves, with our traditions, our history, our
habits, our attitudes, our institutions of democracy and freedom, our general enlightenment,
must have freedom if we are to survive. Only if
we actively encourage discussion, inquiry, and
dissent, only if we put a premium upon nonconformity, can we hope to solve the enormously
complex problems that confront us. Only if we
do this can we enlist the full and grateful support of all our people and command the respect
of our associates abroad.

If in the name of security or of loyalty we
start hacking away at our freedoms — freedom for
the scientist, freedom for the scholar, freedom
for the critic — we will in the end forfeit security
as well. If the commonwealth we cherish is to
survive and prosper, we must encourage free
enterprise in the intellectual and spiritual realms
as well as in the economic. Our responsibility
here is immense. Upon us rests, to a large degree,
the future of Western civilization and of western
Christendom. If we falter here, if by silencing

inquiry and criticism we fall into serious error, the whole of civilization as we know it may go down with us. We must use all our resources and use them wisely. And of all our resources, the richest are in the minds and the spirits of free men. These we must not fritter away. At a time when we are deeply concerned with calculations of strength, we will do well to recall the closing lines of Wordsworth's sonnet, *To Toussaint L'Ouverture:*

> . . . thou hast great allies;
> Thy friends are exaltations, agonies,
> And love, and man's unconquerable mind.

II

The Necessity of Experimentation

In his First Inaugural Address, President Washington observed that 'the preservation of the sacred fire of liberty and the destiny of the republican model of government are justly considered, perhaps, as deeply, as finally, staked on the experiment intrusted to the hands of the American people.' In a very real sense, the whole of our history has been an experiment, even a conscious experiment. For, as Lewis Mumford reminds us, the settlement of America had its origins in the unsettlement of Europe, and this in far more than a merely physical sense. America could not be found, could not emerge out of the mists of the West, until the European mind and culture had dis-integrated and re-integrated, until Europeans had challenged the notions and assumptions of a thousand years or more, and

38

experimented with new techniques and new ideas.

From the beginning, too, our own history was rooted in dissent. The decision to leave England for the New World, the decision to break with community, with church, even with the state (for the break here came before Independence) was a manifestation of an adventurous and experimental attitude. 'Wee hope to plant a nation, where none before hath been,' wrote an early Virginia chronicler, and while the term 'nation' had not then the meaning it has today, this was nevertheless one of the 'prophetic voices concerning America.' But it was a prophecy whose fulfillment depended on the willingness of successive generations to take a chance. So, too, with the waves of westward migrations, to the frontier of Virginia, to the Narragansett Plantations and the Connecticut River, to the Pennsylvania wilderness and beyond, across the Alleghenies and the prairies and the plains and mountains of the west, to the Pacific — all these were expressions of the adventurous pioneering spirit which we celebrate today — but not by imitation.

What was true in a material sense — that the American character was bold and experimental

— was true equally in a philosophical sense. Thus the experiment of nationalism, of the federal system, of a new colonial system, of the separation of church and state, of the practice of democracy and of equality. We take all of these for granted now, because we have been their beneficiaries for over a century, but in their day they were the boldest of gambles.

We take for granted, too, that English language and institutions should prevail over the largest and most flourishing part of this continent. Yet who would have thought this in 1500 or 1600 or even in 1700? Certainly the expansion of this little island, meager alike in resources and population, over the whole of the globe is one of the most astonishing chapters in the history of mankind. Why, after all, did the English succeed where the more powerful French and Spanish failed? There are many reasons for this triumph, but perhaps the fundamental one was that English expansion was an individual or corporate affair rather than a governmental one, and that it was an expression of nonconformity rather than of governmental policy. Unlike its rivals, the English government was willing to take a chance — to permit dissenters to migrate

to colonies, for example; to permit congregations
or joint stock companies to manage colonization;
to permit a large degree of economic and political autonomy. Enterprise, individualism, experimentation, and pluralism characterized English expansion to America, as they were later to
characterize American expansion westward.

That the American people are ingenious, practical, adventurous, and experimental, few will
deny. Nature itself has imposed on us the necessity of invention and experimentation; our national heroes are inventors — Franklin, for example, or Jefferson, equally inventive with tools
or with ideas. We have always been happiest
when we could discover a mechanical solution to
our most difficult problems: the cotton gin, the
harvester, the steamboat, barbed-wire fencing,
and a thousand other inventions of a practical
character; the federal system, or the homestead
policy, or free public education, or lend-lease, or
Marshall aid in the field of social inventiveness.
Pluralism and experimentation characterize our
social and intellectual institutions. Not content
with a single church, Americans experimented
with scores of them, and American denominationalism is the despair of peoples with a tidier

religious scene. No less illuminating is the variety
in the field of education. Even in 1787 the American states had more colleges than did Britain;
since then the proliferation of colleges, courses,
schools, and departments has gone on apace.

Politics, it will be remarked, furnish an exception to these generalizations. The Declaration
of Independence appealed to the Law of Nature
and Nature's God and to unalienable rights
rooted in the moral nature of man and in the
cosmic system. Our early state constitutions were
designed to provide governments of law, and not
of men; our Federal Constitution, too, was in
essentials a product of Newtonian thinking. In
all this our basic political principles are abso-
lutistic and unitary rather than pragmatic and
pluralistic.

True enough. And it is equally true that one
of the great achievements of the American people
was to adapt a constitutional system of this
character to the changing circumstances of the
nineteenth and twentieth centuries. It was an
achievement that required all the resources of
practicality and ingenuity that the American
people could command. That resourcefulness
revealed itself in three forms. First was 'broad

construction' — reading into such phrases as 'regulation of commerce' or 'all needful rules and regulations' or 'the executive power' such authority as seemed requisite. Where our Presidents were too feeble to insist on such broad construction, our legislatures too unenlightened to develop it, our courts too unimaginative to permit it, we got ourselves into trouble. Second was the growth of the unwritten constitution, of all of those practices and techniques through which much of the ordinary business of government is carried on. Third, an outgrowth of the second, was the development of the political party, itself one of the great American inventions. The result of these and other applications of American resourcefulness was a workable Constitution.

The importance of superimposing organic political practices upon static constitutional principles, of the development of an evolutionary and experimental political system out of a rigid constitutional framework, can best be seen in terms of the prolonged controversy over the nature of the Union. One school of political thought — the school whose master was John C. Calhoun — insisted that what the Union was in 1776 or

perhaps in 1787, that it must ever remain; that
man and history were made for political theory
and must conform to it. It insisted that the
states were originally sovereign, had never sur-
rendered their sovereignty, and thus remained
sovereign, and that as sovereignty was absolute,
the states had all sovereignty and the United
States none. Under the lead first of Calhoun,
then of Jefferson Davis, Southerners who had
already closed their minds on the issue of slavery
now closed their minds on the issue of the nature
of the Union. On both of these great issues they
took refuge in abstractions and absolutes. Not-
withstanding the course of American history
since 1787, they insisted that Iowa and Arkansas,
for example, were sovereign because South Caro-
lina and Virginia had been sovereign; and required the loyalty of newly arrived Irish and
German immigrants to the state rather than to
the nation. Historical experience made no im-
pression on the adamantine surface of these
theories: as late as 1881 Jefferson Davis could
write of 'the fictitious idea of *one* people of the
United States,' that 'no such political community
or corporate unit as one people of the United
States has ever been organized, or yet exists; that

no political action by the people of the United States in the aggregate has ever taken place, or ever can take place, under the Constitution.'

From the theoretical point of view this conclusion is logical enough, for on the basis of those absolutist principles which we are now invited to accept, the states were sovereign and remained sovereign! Even from the historical point of view the conclusion is not so much absurd as anachronistic. After all there was no reason to suppose that the independent states of 1776 could or would become one nation, and the subsequent triumph of unity over particularism that made possible a single nation the size of a continent, was unprecedented in history.

How was American nationalism in fact achieved? It was achieved in part, at least, by permitting the widest degree of diversity and experimentation within the larger constitutional framework. It was achieved by a distribution of governmental powers within the federal system and by permitting the states to serve as experimental laboratories. It was achieved by the growth of regional and sectional economies that supplemented and complemented each other and by making them interdependent. It was achieved by encouraging voluntary associations that bound class to class and interest to interest across the nation. It was achieved by permitting and encouraging the widest diversity in religion and in culture — a diversity dramatized by the separation of church and state, and by denominationalism.

Those who insisted that American nationalism was a product of history rather than a repudiation of theory, and who resolutely set about to defend it on that basis, and to help keep it a reality, were not men disposed to abandon either philosophy or morality. Indeed in the first great test of nationalism, the crisis of the 'fifties, absolutism was being used to defend the institution of human slavery, as so often before and since absolutism has been invoked to justify some comparable monstrosity.

The conflict between the absolutist way of looking at things and the experimental, the theoretical, and the pragmatic does not belong wholly to the distant past. It was, philosophically, the heart of the matter in the great controversies of the 1930's. For President Roosevelt's policies, it will not be denied, were opportunistic and experimental; whether they were wanting in moral values, as some critics now assert, is a question that can safely be left to history. Rejecting such concepts as 'rugged individualism,' 'private enterprise,' or 'regimentation' as necessarily cosmic in authority, Roosevelt addressed himself to 'plural and experimental methods in securing . . . an ever-increasing release of the powers of human nature in service of a freedom which is co-operative and a co-operation which is voluntary.' Perhaps the best example of just such an experimental method was the Tennessee Valley Authority, and the best illustration, too, of the antithesis between absolutism and pragmatism in politics. 'For the government deliberately to go out and build up a power business,' said President Hoover in a classic veto message,

'is to break down the initiative and enterprise of the American people; it is the destruction of equality of opportunity of our people; it is the negation of the ideals upon which our civilization has been based . . . it is not liberalism, it is degeneration.'

That President Hoover was entitled to this opinion in 1931 nobody will deny. But what shall we say of those who still insist on the validity of these arguments, twenty years later?

Twenty years is a long time in the history of a
young nation, and there has been ample time to
test President Hoover's assumptions and pre-
dictions. Have the American people in fact
forfeited their initiative and enterprise? Has the
TVA in fact destroyed equality of opportunity
in America? Have we degenerated?

* * * *

'You seem desirous of knowing what Progress
we make here in improving our Governments,'
wrote Benjamin Franklin to his English friend
Jonathan Shipley, in 1786. 'We are, I think, in
the right Road of Improvement, for we are making Experiments. I do not oppose all that seem
wrong, for the Multitude are more effectually set
right by Experience, than kept from going wrong
by Reasoning with them.'

One of the gravest dangers that confronts us
today is the temptation to reject the long tradition of experimentation — the tradition of taking
risks, of gambling on the intelligence, the forti-
tude, the virtue of the American people — and
embrace instead an illusive security. It is not
difficult to understand the yearning for security
that has come over us, but if we suppose that

we can achieve security by resort to the familiar, the traditional, the dogmatic, the absolute, we delude ourselves. If we suppose that we can somehow exact guarantees from history or from God, we delude ourselves.

We want guarantees that all of our teachers in schools and professors in colleges and universities conform to our notions of loyalty and of Americanism, forgetting that those societies — like Nazi Germany and Communist Russia — that enforce conformity on educators make irremediable mistakes, and that those societies like the English, the Scandinavian, the Swiss, and — so far — our own, which protect the freedom of the student and the teacher and the scholar, survive and flourish.

We want guarantees that our children will not be exposed to dangerous ideas, or even to 'controversial' ideas, forgetting that all ideas are dangerous and that only by familiarity with ideas can children ever become adults capable of distinguishing between the true and the false.

We want guarantees that every immigrant is pure in character and in mind, and we subject every potential immigrant to a most rigorous examination of mind, character, and morals, forgetting that all of us are immigrants or the descendants of immigrants, and that neither the Pilgrims nor the Puritans, with their records of nonconformity and lawlessness, could obtain visas today.

We want guarantees that all our organizations are patriotic and loyal in membership and in purpose, forgetting that few of the organizations that carried through the major reforms of our history, from the Puritan Church and the Revolutionary Committees on Correspondence to the Populist party or the Committee to Aid the Allies, of recent years, could pass our current tests, and forgetting, too, how the Quakers, the Baptists, the Unitarians, the Catholics all suffered persecution and harassment for their heterodoxy, in the past.

We want guarantees that no power granted by our Constitution can ever be abused, and distinguished statesmen point with alarm to the fact that the treaty-making power is a power 'subject to abuse,' forgetting that almost every power granted in the Constitution is subject to abuse — including the legislative — but that in a century and a half no treaty has ever yet been held to violate a provision of the Constitution; and forgetting, too, that if the proposed Bricker Amendment had been in effect early enough we could not even have concluded the treaty that gave us our independence.

In short we want security and certainty, forgetting that 'certainty is an illusion,' and forgetting, too, what Justice Holmes has admonished us, that 'the constitution is an experiment, as all life is an experiment,' and that 'every day we have to wager our salvation upon some prophecy based upon imperfect knowledge.'

Does all this mean that we are losing confidence in the next generation, and its successors, and looking to earlier generations for our salvation? Does it mean that we are forgetting what was once instinctive with us, that each generation must validate old truth and discover new truth for itself, and that each generation is as capable of doing this as were past generations? Does it mean that we think that we are the people and all wisdom dies with us? that we have put behind us that concept expressed so nobly by Isaac Newton when he described himself as a child sitting on the beach playing with sand and pebbles while all about him stretched the vast ocean of truth?

Does it mean that we have forgotten, or have failed to learn, what might be called the first lesson of pragmatism: damn the absolute! For increasingly we take refuge in abstractions, not in realities. We fall back on clichés and stereotypes, on words like regimentation, bureaucracy, creeping socialism, left wing, private enterprise, American system, rugged individualism, fellow-traveler, appeasement, and we assume that these words are expressions of thought when they are for the most part declarations of intellectual bankruptcy. We succumb to the techniques of the advertisers and drain familiar words of meaning, saying with Humpty-Dumpty, 'When I use a word it means just what I choose it to mean,' and thus forfeit words that have had dignity: loyalty, liberalism, freedom, for example. We surrender to those whom George Eliot has called the 'men of maxims':

'All people of broad, strong sense have an instinctive repugnance to the men of maxims; because such people early discover that the mysterious complexity of our life is not to be embraced by maxims, and that to lace ourselves up in formulas of that sort is to repress all the divine promptings and inspirations that spring from growing insight and sympathy. And the man of maxims is the popular representative of the minds that are guided in their moral judgments solely by general rules, thinking that these will lead them to justice by ready-made patent method, without the trouble of exerting patience, discrimination, impartiality, without any care to assure themselves whether they have the insight that comes from a hardly-earned estimate of temptation, or from a life vivid and intense enough to have created a wide fellow-feeling with all that is human.'

It is the pragmatist who stands in sharpest contrast to the man of maxims — the pragmatist who (and I am quoting William James) 'seeks to determine the meaning of all difference of opinion by making the discussion hinge as soon as possible upon some practical or particular issue.'

It is when we resolutely insist that the discussions should hinge as soon as possible upon some particular issue that we discover the fallacies of the doctrinaire or absolutist approach to the great problems now confronting us. For everyone agrees that loyalty is better than disloyalty, that freedom is preferable to slavery, truth to error. It is only when we come to examine these words, or these concepts, in relation to actual situations

that we are able to make intelligent choices. It
is then that we appreciate the importance, nay
the necessity, of that approach which William
James has described in one of his most memorable passages:

'Grant an idea or belief to be true, what concrete
difference will its being true make in anyone's
actual life? How will the truth be realized? What
experiences will be different from those which
would obtain if the belief were false? The moment pragmatism asks this question, it sees the
answer. True ideas are those we can assimilate,
validate, corroborate, and verify. False ideas are
those that we cannot.'

This attitude toward truth and conduct, and
their relations, is today under very heavy attack.
Truth, it is argued, is not relative but absolute;
truth is universal and *a priori,* and not to be
subjected to the hazards of experimental tests.
Truth is not something to be made and remade
by erring man; it is rather something that is
rooted in the very nature of things. The most
severe criticism of pragmatism, then, is that it
appears to rationalize the notion that truth may
shift around from day to day to serve the conve-
nience of those who invoke it, or the no less
odious notion that the end justifies the means.

This criticism of pragmatism, which in some form dates back to its earliest formulation, came to a head in the striking chapter called 'The Pragmatic Acquiescence' in Lewis Mumford's *Golden Day*. Pragmatism, Mumford charged, had acquiesced in the vulgarization of manners and morals, in elevating to respectability the cash-value principle of morality, in subordinating ends to means.

Now there is something very naïve about this, and about much subsequent criticism which echoes it. One might suppose that values were a monopoly of the *a priori* school, that no one had ever thought of them before these critics took up the cudgels on their behalf. Or one might suppose that William James and John Dewey were the willing tools of the powers that be, of the business civilization or the political bosses whose petty malpractices required some sort of philosophical whitewash. Certainly it is easy to sympathize with James himself when he protested that 'The pragmatism that lives inside of me is so different from that of which I succeed in wakening the idea inside of other people, that theirs makes me feel like cursing God and dying.' For pragmatism is primarily an ethical

attitude, and James and Dewey were primarily
ethical leaders. Far from being acquiescent,
James was an instinctive and congenital rebel.
His mind, wrote George Santayana, was like the
Polish constitution — a single negative vote, and
the question remained open indefinitely. He
was, above all, the philosopher of the open mind
and the affluent spirit, of the endless search for
values and for truth. He did not commit the
vulgar error of supposing that there could be
value without experience, or experience without
value; only minds dead to experience, and to
life itself, can entertain such notions. As for
Dewey, he, too, was a protestant, a rebel, and a
come-outer, a dreamer of dreams with a Yankee's
talent for materializing them into institutions
and practices.

And it is proper to ask, too, who has acquiesced? Who acquiesced in the defense of the
status quo, those who took refuge in the absolute
and axiomatic character of the economic principles of Herbert Spencer and the constitutional
principles of Justice Field, or those who protested against absolutes in economics and in law
and fought for change and improvement? We
can profitably broaden the question to embrace

the great philosophical crisis of our own time. Which peoples, in the crucial struggles of the 1930's and 1940's, ranged themselves on the side of the preservation of the great moral values of Western Christendom; which devoted themselves to the repudiation and destruction of those values? It was not the people trained through generations to belief in 'absolutes' — the people who took as cosmic truths the natural superiority of Aryan over Jew, or of the state over man — who fought for the permanent values of our civilization. These, on the contrary, seemed to find it easy enough to set up their Buchenwalds and Belsens to enforce their own absolutes and eradicate dissenters. It was rather the British and the Americans, the peoples supposedly abandoned to pragmatism and without a proper sense of moral values, who fought for freedom and the dignity of man. The notion that pragmatism acquiesces readily in materialism and is blind to moral values is a notion that ignores history and experience.

Persecution — not only the comparatively mild persecution of our own time and our own country by investigating committees or private black-lists or social ostracism, but the persecution of

rack and of stake — is the logical product of the
absolutist, not of the pragmatic, temper. For, as
Justice Holmes observed in *Abrams* v. *United
States:*

'persecution for the expression of opinions seems
to me perfectly logical. If you have no doubt
of your premises or of your power and want a
certain result with all your heart, you naturally
express your wishes in law and sweep away all
opposition. To allow opposition by speech seems
to indicate that you think the speech impotent, as
when a man says he has squared the circle, or
that you do not care whole-heartedly for the
result, or that you doubt either your power or
your premises.'

As Holmes suggests, granted the premises, persecution is logical and practical. A society that
already possesses the whole of truth has no need
for further truth, and properly silences those who
submit unorthodox ideas. If Senator McCarthy
knows what is the whole of loyalty, he rightly
regards anyone who departs from his standards
as engaged in a foolish or a criminal activity. If
Dean Clarence Manion knows the whole truth
about private enterprise and governmental regulation, he quite logically regards experimenta-
tions in this realm as pernicious, and has no need

to await the findings of a Commission before he denounces the TVA. If those Far Eastern experts, Senators Ferguson and Knowland, know the whole truth, future as well as past, about China, they are entirely right in their unqualified hostility toward the present government, and in regarding not only the Lattimores and Fairbankses of the academic world but the Achesons and Marshalls of the political world as dupes or marplots. If Governors Talmadge and Byrnes know all that can be known about the purposes of God and Nature in making some men white and others black, then they are entirely right in regarding those who encourage the equality of the races as persons engaged in immoral activities. But to all of those who are certain of the validity of their own beliefs and faiths and values, and certain that they share these with the cosmos, we can but repeat Justice Holmes's warning:

'When men have realized that time has upset many fighting faiths, they may come to believe even more than they believe the very foundations of their own conduct, that the ultimate good desired is better reached by free trade in ideas.'

* * * *

In our own time the attack upon pragmatism has focused on education and law. Pragmatism is equated with 'progressive education' and all the vagaries of our most 'progressive' school systems are ascribed, in turn, to pragmatism. That schools teach cooking and tap dancing and automobile driving rather than Latin and mathematics is blamed, in some obscure way, on William James and John Dewey. Because Dewey insisted that education was not divorced from life but was part of life; because he urged that teaching be associated with doing, so that children could learn the relation between abstract knowledge and work; because he rejected a uniform and standard curriculum, or reliance upon traditional subjects as valid for all students and all purposes, he is marked down as the godfather of every eccentricity conceived in the mind of the most shallow-minded educationalist.

That our grade and high schools fail to educate, in the sense that the English public school, the French lycée, the German gymnasium educate, will readily be admitted, nor will it be denied that they have failed to produce that urbane, civilized, and open-minded citizenry which is the ideal of most educators. For this situation there are, needless to say, explanations and extenuations. If I should attempt to state the explanation in a single sentence, it would be this: that in America we have required our schools to perform many functions aside from the academic, and that the task of mass education for democratic and equalitarian conditions cannot be performed as well as the task of selective education for a highly specialized class society. If I were to state the extenuating circumstance in a single sentence it would be this: that our schools faithfully reflect our own society, and that a society which rewards motion-picture stars more highly than scholars or scientists, and features football games on the front page of its papers, can scarcely expect its schools to inculcate different standards and values.

That the failings of education in America are egregious is beyond dispute. That they are more egregious than the failings of French or German education is by no means clear. It is relevant to remember, what bemused critics of American and admirers of European education so often forget, that the highly educated products of the German gymnasia succumbed readily enough to the anti-intellectualism of the Nazis, and that a substantial segment of the French intelligensia

gave way to defeatism in the crisis of the 'forties.
The British record here was very different, but
again it is relevant to note that Britain has long
been abandoned to empiricism, and that British
education, from the lowest forms through the
universities, has long flourished in an atmosphere
of freedom.

What is, however, clear is that the failings of
American education that now inspire most vociferous criticism are not those which can be
properly traced to the experimental method or
to the pragmatic philosophy. There is nothing
about pragmatism that discourages the study of
Greek and mathematics and encourages the study
of salesmanship and typewriting in our schools
and colleges. Quite the contrary. If the accumu-
lated experience of Western man shows — as it
may well — that men trained in classics and
mathematics (that is, trained as the Founding
Fathers were trained, or as the top British civil
service is trained) do a better job in the profes-
sions, in business, in government, than those
exposed to vocational training, then pragmatism
will logically call for a return to the classical
curriculum.

What is dangerous is not the experimental

method, but the chance that a particular experiment be mistaken for Natural Law, a result equally dangerous whether it suggests that all of our problems will be solved by the compulsory study of 'citizenship' or the compulsory study of Thomas Aquinas. What is dangerous is not the insistence upon values, but the risk that the temporary and selfish values of a particular group or interest or section be mistaken for permanent, universal, and cosmic values. What is dangerous is not that schools should be called upon to serve the community, but that they be made instruments for the advancement of local or private interests rather than instruments for inculcating the love of truth and the search for it.

Only less dangerous than the attack on progressive education is the attack upon sociological jurisprudence and the revival of Natural Law. As the criticism of progressivism in education is focused on John Dewey, so the criticism of sociological jurisprudence is focused on Justice Oliver Wendell Holmes. Listen, for example, to Mr. Henry Luce as he dedicated the Dallas Law Center:

'I submit to you today that we ought to believe what is true, and that the truth is that we live

in a moral universe, that the laws of this country
and of any country are invalid and will be in
fact inoperative except as they conform to a
moral order which is universal in time and space.
Holmes held that what I have just said is untrue,
irrelevant, and even dangerous.'

Certainly Holmes held that the argument here
set forth was irrelevant, and not Holmes alone.
He would not have been inclined to challenge
the argument that we ought to believe what is
true, but he would certainly have asked for the
credentials of those who presumed to pronounce
truth. To the observation that we live in a moral
universe, he would probably have asked whose
morality it was that was to be proclaimed universal, and he would certainly have added one
of his most familiar remarks, that the first step
in wisdom was to learn that you were not God,
and that he saw no reason to identify his own
'can't helps' with those of the universe. 'I prefer
champagne to ditch-water,' he said, 'but I have
no reason to suppose that the cosmos does.'

The argument that laws are inoperative unless
they conform to a moral order is, of course, a
very old and respectable one. It was supposed
to be one of the fundamental principles of the

British constitutional system; it animated the
fathers of the Revolution and of the Constitution; and it made a decisive contribution to the
practice of judicial review. It was a great and
noble concept; the trouble came — as it did come
— with its application. For who was to delineate
the moral order to which laws were to conform,
and who was to determine conformity or nonconformity? To the New England Federalists
the moral order, written into the Constitution,
forbade the purchase of Louisiana; to Southern
slave-holders it required the protection of slavery
in all the territories of the United States, while to
Abolitionists it justified almost any assault upon
the peculiar institution or even on the Constitution which appeared to vindicate it. For from
the beginning judges had read their own preconceptions about economy and politics into
the Constitution and identified this reading with
the moral order; with the Fourteenth Amendment this judicial practice came to be regular-
ized. As guardians of universal moral truths
judges saw to it that legislatures did not interfere
too roughly with those economic and social practices which Nature had decreed. It was contrary
to the moral law, so they discovered, to prevent

women from working ten hours in a factory if
they so pleased, or to deny them the right to
work through the night. It was contrary to the
moral law to limit the hours of labor in bake-
shops to sixty a week, or to prohibit tobacco
manufacture in the home, for — as one of the
judges said — 'it cannot be perceived how the
cigar maker is to be improved in his health or
his morals by forcing him from his home and its
hallowed associations and beneficent influences
to ply his trade elsewhere.' It was contrary to
the moral law to limit returns on an investment
to a meager six per cent or to permit the United
States to collect any income tax, or to fix mini-
mum wages for women in industry.

It is unnecessary to elaborate on anything so
familiar, and I recall these episodes in our history
merely to suggest that while all agree on the
desirability of a universal moral law, few agree
on the particular character of the law, or on its
application. To those who are confident that
they can be trusted with the responsibility of
interpreting and applying moral law, it is an
edifying thought that the Supreme Court has
reversed itself on every one of the interpretations
cited above.

In a country such as ours, with so many racial, religious, and sectional groups, and with forty-eight political laboratories, it would be all but fatal to insist on conformity to absolutes — the absolutes of constitutionalism, or of politics, or of economics. What Holmes said three-quarters of a century ago, in his lectures on the Common Law, is still valid:

'The life of the law has not been logic; it has been experience. The felt necessities of the time, the prevalent moral and political theories, intuitions of public policy, avowed or unconscious, even the prejudices which judges share with their fellow men, have had a good deal more to do than the syllogism in determining the rules by which men should be governed.'

He was describing the evolution of the Common Law. It is pertinent to note that in Germany and Italy, Spain and France, which inherited the traditions of the Roman law — a law which was comprehensive and codified — the rights of subjects have not always been safeguarded, but in England, whose law broadened down from precedent to precedent, the liberties of the subject have been as safe as anywhere on the globe.

But let us return to our original theme. That

is, not so much **Damn** the absolute! — a negative
attitude after all — as exalt and encourage the
experimental! Exalt the open mind, tolerance,
faith in progress and in the ability of men and
women to conquer new worlds of science and
politics and economy, to discover new truths of
philosophy. We must encourage the experimental attitude in science — as we for the most
part do — because if we create a climate of
opinion in which scientists fear to be bold and
original or if we require that they work only on
projects that appear to be of immediate importance to us, we shall end up with scientists and
scientific knowledge inadequate to the tasks that
we impose upon them. This is what happened in
Nazi Germany and it is one of the reasons why
the Nazis lost the war. We must encourage experimentation in politics — as in the past we
have — because only if we realize that politics is
not a closed but an open system, that there is
room not only for improvements in the machinery but for new principles and new machinery, can we hope to adapt the existing
political system to the crowding problems which
we ask it to solve. If we close the avenues of
political experimentation, whether by imposing

intellectual conformity on our civil service, or by discouraging independence in our diplomats, or by such a tightening up of the Constitution as is explicit in the two-term amendment or the proposed Bricker Amendment — we shall find that our political machinery will grind to a stop. Experience should teach us to leave to such countries as Italy, Germany, Spain, Russia, and their imitators self-indulgence in closed political systems. We must encourage experimentation in the economy — as for the most part we do — because the heavy responsibilties that have come to us as the economic leaders of the Western world require that we keep our minds and our machinery flexible and resourceful. We must realize that if we equate the American system with 'private enterprise' and 'private enterprise' with hostility to the TVA or a federal housing program or a public-health program, we shall saddle private enterprise with an intolerable burden and expose the American system itself to grave danger. For the only enterprise that is really private is intellectual enterprise, and upon this depends all other enterprise; the only American habit that can really be called a system is the habit of pluralism and experimentation.

We must encourage experimentation in international relations, because the problems of
world politics and world leadership are infinitely
complex and are fluid. If we commit ourselves
irretrievably to a single course of action or a
single program, we may find that we have built
a prison wall around ourselves. We must leave
room for maneuver and for the traditional give
and take of the conference table, or we shall
imperil our title to world leadership. 'It is a
mistake,' Sir Winston Churchill has written,

'to try to write out on little pieces of paper what
the vast emotions of an outraged and quivering
world will be either immediately after the
struggle is over, or when the inevitable cold fit
follows the hot. These awe-inspiring tides of
feeling dominate most people's minds, and independent figures tend to become not only lonely
but futile. Guidance in these mundane matters
is granted to us only step by step, or at the utmost
a step or two ahead. There is therefore wisdom
is reserving one's decisions as long as possible,
and until all the facts and forces that will be
potent at the moment are revealed' (*Triumph
and Tragedy*).

We must therefore look with grave misgivings
upon the psychology of the 'crusade' or on the

notion that we can make the world over in our image either by persuasion or by coercion.

We must encourage experimentation even in the moral realm, for even if it is true, as it well may be, that some moral values are so fundamental that we can properly call them universal, it is still possible to find new meanings and new applications in old truths — new meaning and new reality in the concepts of freedom, for example, or of the dignity of the human being. For practical purposes we must and do consider many questions as closed; we do not, after all, experiment with the multiplication table, or with driving eighty miles an hour on a highway. But in the moral realm we are enjoined not only to hold fast that which is good, but to prove all things. And it is the same St. Paul who has reminded us that 'God hath not given us the spirit of fear; but of power, and of love, and of a sound mind.'

III

Free Enterprise in Ideas

'I SOMETIMES THINK that when folks talk about things they've begun to lose them already,' says Stark Young's Hugh McGehee to his son after an evening of Southern rodomontade. It would be an exaggeration to say that we have begun to lose liberty in America, but it is sobering that there should be so much talk about it, just as it is sobering that there should be so much talk about Americanism and about loyalty. It was a happier time when these things could be taken for granted instead of being soiled and worn by every sunshine patriot eager for cheap applause. Nor is much of the talk itself resassuring. Liberty is enlisted in strange armies, pressed into service for curious causes, and as we listen to some of the arguments for censorship or exclusion or suppression, all in the name of liberty, we are reminded irresistibly of Madame Roland's cry on the scaffold, 'Liberty, what crimes are done in thy name.'

Nor is the difficulty wholly with those who, in a sort of vindication of Orwell's *1984,* invoke liberty for oppression. Some of the difficulty comes from well-intentioned idealists who are content with familiar formulas, or who would interpret liberty as wholly a personal and individual affair — a matter of abstract principle rather than of conduct, of private rights rather than of general social responsibilities.

When we consider civil and political liberties we must avoid the pleasant illusions of abstractions and get down to cases. We must look to the meaning of our freedoms in their present-day context, and in their operation. And when we do this we must remember what Harold Laski so insistently urged upon us (in *Reflections on the Revolution of Our Time*), that rights and liberties do not mean the same thing to all of us:

'The rule of law is a principle with a fairly long history behind it. And if the burden of that history has one outstanding lesson it is that, over the social process as a whole, the rule of law is only equally applied as between persons

. . . whose claim on the state power is broadly
recognized as equal. The rule of law is not an
automatic principle of action which operates
indifferently as to time and place and the persons
to whom, as judges, its application is entrusted.
It is very likely to be one thing for a Negro in
Georgia and another thing for a white man in
Georgia.'

The function of freedom — let us say of the guarantee of due process or of the right to vote — for
the Negro and the white in the South is one
very obvious example of why we have to look to
the operation of the principle rather than to its
mere formulation. Others come readily to mind:
the difference in guarantees of freedom to white
and to Oriental during World War II, for example, or the different treatment afforded the
vagrant and the respectable citizen, or that difference in the attitude toward corporate crime and
individual crime which Professor Sutherland has
explored in his study of *White Collar Crime*.

We must recognize, too, at the outset that
there are two very broad categories of violations
of liberty: the political and the nonpolitical, or
perhaps we should say the official and the unofficial. Only the first has received adequate atten-

tion — invasion of personal rights by the federal
or state governments or by some administrative
body. These are the impairments of liberty that
are dramatized in the press and challenged in the
courts — a flag-salute law, a segregation law, a
white primary law, the censorship of a film, or
the administrative seizure of an industry. Yet
the second category of invasion and impairment,
the unofficial, is more widespread and more
effective than the first. It is invasion by social
or community pressure, by the pressure of public
opinion or of public customs and habits — the
kind of invasion that Tocqueville described and
warned against over a century ago. It is very
difficult to get at this by law. Fair Employment
Practice Acts may prevent a Negro or a Jew from
getting fired for racial reasons, but they will not
go far toward getting him a job in the first place.
A teacher who has been guilty of dangerous
thoughts can take a broken contract to court, but
she cannot deal with community pressure that
makes it advisable for her to move on, nor can
she force other school boards to give her a job.
We have only to read Norman Cousins' description * of the interplay of social and economic

* *Saturday Review*, 3 May 1952.

pressures in Peoria, Illinois, to realize how enormously effective these are and how difficult it is to do anything about them. As John Stuart Mill observed a century ago, 'The immense mass of mankind are, in regard to their usages, in a state of social slavery; each man being bound under heavy penalties to conform to the standard of life common to his own class.'

Our basic freedoms, in short, are not as basic as we like to think, just as our passion for individualism is not as passionate as we suppose. If we content ourselves with abstractions we may go seriously astray; as Professor Denis Brogan has remarked in his recent book on revolutions, the American claim to — and hope for — a special place in the affections of Asian peoples is frustrated by the elementary fact that of all the powers of the world 'America is the most color conscious.' We may believe that our words — which we assume to express our principles — represent us more truly even than our actions, but to outsiders it is the actions that are more eloquent than the words.

Now it will be granted at once that our traditional liberties are not absolute — not in a mathematical sense, anyway. All of them are qualified by the rights of society, or of the state. There are limits on liberty, as there are limits on authority. The broad principle of those limits is generally recognized and accepted; no liberties may be exercised so as to injure others, or injure the community.

Needless to say, this does not get us very far. That liberty is not absolute is one of those truisms that is almost always brought out and put to work whenever somebody wants to censor a book or a film that he doesn't like, or to throw a teacher or a librarian or a radio performer out of his job. Actually it is worth stating only as an introduction to the real problems. How do we determine the limits on liberty and the rights and interests of the community? And who are the 'we' who determine? It is easy to fall back on the generalization that the freedom of the individual must not be used to injure the community, and easy enough to say that in the last analysis it is society which determines. But these vague answers are of no practical help. To draw the line between the exercise of freedom and the limitations on freedom is one of the most delicate tasks of statesmanship and philosophy. And the power of drawing the line is one of the

most complex and sobering exercises of political
authority.

It is in the drawing of lines, the setting of
boundaries, the fixing of limits, the reconciliation of claims that the problems rise. Look where
we will, in our own society we will find that
problems of freedom or of rights revolve around
this matter of fixing limits and drawing lines.
Thus in the conflicting claims of a free press and
a responsible press, or of freedom and license in
the press. Thus in the conflicting claims of
liberty and security in diplomacy, or in science.
Thus in the conflicting claims of artistic freedom
and of the protection of the morals of the community, or of religious freedom and protection
against blasphemy or the stirring up of religious
hatreds. Thus in the conflicting claims of the
right to public entertainment and the right to
privacy. Thus in the conflicting claims of the
right to private organization and the interest
of society in protecting itself against dangerous
organizations. Thus in the conflicting claims of
conscience — let us say of conscientious objectors
to military service or a flag salute — and of national defense or of patriotism. Thus in the
conflicting claims of academic freedom and of the

right of a democracy to determine what should be taught in its schools — and how.

Now we have been using the word 'conflicting' somewhat uncritically. But is not the conflict exaggerated, and have we searched intensively enough for the reconciliation? We must keep in mind that the community has a paramount interest in the rights of the individual, and the individual a paramount interest in the welfare of the community of which he is a part. The community cannot prosper without permitting, nay encouraging, the far-reaching exercise of individual freedom; the individual cannot be safe without permitting, nay supporting, the far-reaching exercise of authority by the state.

There is, in short, too much emphasis on independence and not enough on interdependence; too much emphasis on division and not enough on unity. Actually it is only to the superficial view that there is any genuine conflict between liberty and security, for example, or between academic freedom and social freedom.

For what is clear on closer examination is that we cannot have any one of these alleged goods without the other. There is no real choice between freedom and security. Only those societies that actively encourage freedom — that encourage, for example, scientific and scholarly research, the questioning of scientific and social orthodoxies and the discovery of new truths — only such societies can hope to solve the problems that assail them and preserve their security. The experience of Nazi Germany is all but conclusive on this (we are still required to wait until all the returns are in from Russia, but it is a reasonable prophecy that Russia will fall behind on scientific and social research just as Germany did). A nation that silences or intimidates original minds is left only with unoriginal minds and cannot hope to hold its own in the competition of peace or of war. As John Stuart Mill said in that essay on 'Liberty' to which we cannot too often repair, 'A state which dwarfs its men, in order that they may be more docile instruments in its hands . . . will find that with small men no great thing can really be accomplished.'

It is probable that other alleged alternatives so vehemently urged upon us are equally fictitious. Take, for example, the matter of the claims of 'academic freedom' and of a society concerned with the teaching of truth — as is every sound society. Clearly there is no genuine conflict here. All but the most thoughtless or the most ignorant know that unless education is free the minds of the next generation will be enslaved. Even in American Legion halls it is probably a bust of Socrates that stands in the niche — Socrates who was condemned because he was a corruptor of youth — rather than of those forgotten members of the tribunal who put him to death. We have always known that academic freedom, like other freedoms, was subject to abuse, but we have also known (up to now, in any event) that the abuse was part of the price paid for the use, and that it was not in fact a high price. The simple fact is that the kind of society that cherishes academic freedom is the kind that gets the best teachers and scholars and students, and the kind that tries to control what teachers may teach or students learn is the kind that ends up with mediocre teachers and mediocre students. A comparison of German science and scholarship in the generation before the First World War and the generation of Nazism should be conclusive on this.

So, too, with the problem of freedom of the press as against the right of the community to

protect itself against libel or obscenity or sedition
or against similar dangers. Granted that there is
no absolute freedom of the press — no right to
proclaim blasphemy to church-goers or to distri-
bute obscene literature to children — the alleged
conflict is still largely fictitious. The hypothetical
dangers linger in the realm of hypothesis; when
they emerge from this to reality they can be dealt
with by ordinary nuisance or libel or criminal
laws, not by censorship laws. We are all familiar
with Justice Holmes's graphic illustration of the
man who cries 'fire' in a crowded theater, but the
fact is that no sane man ever does this, and our
ordinary laws should not be made for the hypothetical insane. The fact is that censorship always
defeats its own purpose, for it creates, in the end,
the kind of society that is incapable of exercising
real discretion, incapable, that is, of doing an
honest or intelligent job, and thus guarantees a
steady intellectual decline.

We must, then, keep in mind that we are
dealing with realities, not abstractions. We must
learn to think things, not words; we must fasten
our attention on consequences, not on theories.
We must keep ever in mind the warning of
William James that meaningful discussion will

'hinge as soon as possible upon some practical or particular issue.'

The importance of this becomes clear when we realize that almost everyone agrees on the principles that should govern our conduct. At least almost all say and probably think that they agree. It is the application that is different. Southerners who deny Negroes a fair trial purport to be enthusiastic for the Bill of Rights but do not apply it in the same way to whites and Negroes. The Legislature of Texas which passed a resolution outlawing any party that 'entertained any thought or principle' contrary to the Constitution of the United States was doubtless sincere enough, but it did not intend to outlaw the Democratic party because that party 'entertains' a thought contrary to the Fifteenth Amendment. Senator McCarthy doubtless thinks of himself as a paladin of Constitutional liberties and so does Senator McCarran; Merwin K. Hart of the National Economic Council and Allen Zook of the notorious National Council for American Education invoke the Constitution, as do the editors of *Counterattack* and of *Red Channels*. All this is too obvious for rehearsal. We must get beyond the principles to their application in order to discover where the difficulty is, and to discover how to resolve it.

When we approach the problem this way we can see that the most compelling argument for freedom is not the argument from theory or principle, but the argument of necessity. To put the issue as simply as possible: we maintain freedom not in order to indulge error but in order to discover truth, and we know no other way of discovering truth. It is difficult to think of any situation where this principle does not apply.

This does not mean for a moment that the principles are unimportant. They are enormously important. They provide the framework of our thinking. They provide us with a common vocabulary. They crystallize for us the values we cherish. If we did not have a body of principles of freedom, we should not be discussing this matter at all. The principles are important, then, and essential. But it is in the application that we discover their meaning. It is the application that is the test. If we are to solve our problems, it must be by traveling the road of conduct and consequences. Theory may mislead us; experience must be our guide

Let us note three or four examples. Here, for instance, is perhaps the most important of all at the moment — the conflicting claims of scientific freedom and national security. To talk in abstract terms of the freedom of the scientist does not get us very far, for that is not an abstract freedom; it is a freedom whose effective exercise requires a good deal of co-operation from the community. Nor does it get us very far to talk in abstract terms about national security. Everyone is in favor of national security, but Senators Morse and McCarthy have different notions about how it is to be achieved. The meaningful approach is that of consequences. What happens when you adopt a policy of freedom for research — freedom with commonsense regulations that any sensible man may be expected to observe? What happens when you permit the Government or the military to control the research? Fortunately, we need not speculate here; Walter Gelhorn's remarkable study of *Security, Loyalty, and Science* has covered the ground and furnished the moral.

'The costs of secrecy [he says] are high. When the freedom of scientific exchange is curtailed, an unfavorable reaction upon further scientific development is inevitable. We pay for secrecy by slowing the rate of our scientific progress, now and in the future. This loss of momentum may conceivably be disastrous, for even from the strictly military point of view "it is just as important for us to have some new secrets to keep as it is for us to hold on to the old ones." If it is unsound to suppress scientific knowledge during the long years of a cold war, the American people may one day discover that they have been crouching behind a protective wall of blueprints and formulas whose impregnability is an utter illusion.'

Or let us look to an equally familiar field — the effort to rid our school system of alleged 'subversives.' Ignore for the moment all questions about the definition of subversive (a term that has not yet been legally defined) or about the rights of teachers. Look solely to the social interest, the community interest, in the matter, and apply the test of consequences. What happens when a state tries to purge its state universities or a community tries to purge its public schools of alleged subversives?

We have a good deal of evidence on this matter by now, for the campaign against subversives has gone on for some time. We can therefore speak here with some assurance. What happens is not that the state or city gets rid of hordes of Communists. Not at all. It very rarely finds any,* and it rarely finds any subversives unless it wants to stretch that term to embrace anyone who rejoiced in Russian victories in 1943 or who reads

* William B. Pendergast of the U.S. Naval Academy thus summarizes the situation as of 1950: 'In none of the states which enacted anti-subversive laws in 1949 was any need for the legislation demonstrated. Texas had one known Communist student in its state universities and colleges. Maryland . . . only one had held any public position in the recent past, and that as a kindergarten teacher in the Baltimore schools; this teacher was dismissed in 1948. . . A survey made by *The New York Times* in September 1949 disclosed that no Communist problem existed in the school systems of twenty-nine of the nation's largest cities. . . Governor Dever of Massachusetts declared that, to his knowledge there were no Communists in the ranks of his state's employees. . . Proponents of the anti-subversive laws here discussed failed to name a single Communist employed by their states in 1949. They failed to cite a single dangerous act recently perpetrated by Communists within their states. Inquiry into the operation of the 1949 legislation . . . confirms the suspicion that there was no pressing need for the legislation. . . Nothing resembling a Communist was turned up anywhere as a result of the operation of these laws. The only tangible effect of the legislation to date has been added work for file clerks who handle the loyalty declarations.' 'State Legislatures and Communism: The Current Scene,' XLIV, *American Political Science Review,* 571-2.

The Nation or who favors socialized medicine.
What happens is the demoralization and the
eventual corruption of the school system. This is
not a momentary or even a temporary affair; it
is something the consequences of which may be
felt for years. The search for subversives results
in the intimidation of the independent, the original, the imaginative, and the experimental-
minded. It discourages independence of thought
in teachers and students alike. It discourages the
joining of organizations that may turn out to be
considered subversive. It discourages the reading of books that may excite the suspicion of
some investigator or some Legionnaire. It discourages criticism of educational or of Governmental policies. It discourages the discussion of
controversial matters in the classroom, for such
discussion may be reported, or misreported, and
cause trouble. It creates a situation where first-
rate minds will not go into teaching or into
administration and where students therefore get
poor teaching. In the long run it will create a
generation incapable of appreciating the difference between independence of thought and subservience. In the long run it will create a

generation not only deprived of liberty but incapable of enjoying liberty.

Turn where we will to apply the test of consequences, we discover that we must insist on freedom because we cannot do without it, because we cannot afford the price of its denial. Thus the most powerful argument against Congressional programs of investigation of Foundations ('To determine if they are using their resources for un-American and subversive activities or for purposes not in the interest or tradition of the United States') is that if it is put into effect it will endanger existing foundations and discourage philanthropists from setting up others and discourage that boldness and independence which foundations can provide more freely than almost any other institution. The most powerful argument against the censorship of textbooks and the elimination of 'un-American' ideas or of anything critical of the 'American spirit of private enterprise' is that such censorship will guarantee the elimination of textbooks with any ideas at all. The compelling argument against the purging of libraries is that if the kind of people who believe in purges have their way and work their will, our libraries will cease to be centers of light and learning and become instead instruments of party or church or class, or depositories of literature whose only merit is its innocuousness. The compelling argument against denying passports or visas on the grounds of unpopular political or economic ideas is that by silencing criticism in those who expect to travel from country to country we deprive ourselves of the value of what foreigners might have to tell us, discourage criticism in our own citizens, and deny to foreigners living evidence that the United States encourages intellectual independence. The decisive argument against the kind of censorship of radio and motion-picture performers that we are now witnessing is that it will leave us, in the end, with programs devoid of ideas and performers devoid of originality or of courage to apply originality.

In every case it is society that is the loser. Our society can doubtless afford to lose the benefits of ideas or character in any one instance, but the cumulative costs of the intimidation of thoughtful and critical men and women is something no society can afford.

A society that applies doctrinaire notions to social conduct will find itself in the end the prisoner of its own doctrines. A society that takes refuge in shibboleths like 'subversive' or 'un-American' will find itself unable to recognize reality when it appears — even the reality of danger. A society that discourages experiment will find that without experiment there can be no progress, and that without progress, there is regress. A society that attempts to put education and science and scholarship in strait jackets will find that in strait jackets there can be no movement, and that the result will be intellectual atrophy. A society that repudiates free enterprise in the intellectual arena under the deluded notion that it can flourish in the economic alone will find that without intellectual enterprise, economic enterprise dries up. A society that encourages state intervention in the realm of ideas will find itself an easy prey to state intervention in other realms as well.

That government which most scrupulously protects and encourages complete freedom of thought, expression, communication, investigation, criticism is the one which has the best chance of achieving security and progress. 'They that can give up essential liberty to obtain a little temporary safety deserve neither liberty nor safety,' wrote Benjamin Franklin two centuries ago, and what he said is as valid now as it was then. Government and society have a paramount interest in independence, originality, heterodoxy, criticism, nonconformity, because all experience teaches that it is out of these that come new ideas, and because every society needs a continuous re-examination of old ideas and a continuous flow of new ideas. And it is relevant to remember, too, that it is nonconformity that needs encouragement. As William Ellery Channing said over a century ago, 'We have conservatives enough.'

Three centuries ago John Milton addressed himself to the problem that now confronts us, and what he said in *Areopagitica* is still valid:

'Believe it, Lords and Commons, they who counsel ye to such a suppressing do as good as bid ye suppress yourselves. . . Ye cannot make us now less capable, less knowing, less eagerly pursuing of the truth, unless ye first make yourselves, that made us so, less the lovers, less the founders of our true liberty.'

IV

Guilt by Association?

GUILT BY ASSOCIATION is very old — and so, too,
the protest against it. Most of you will recall
the admonitions of the prophet Ezekiel: 'What
mean ye, that ye use this proverb concerning the
land of Israel, saying "The fathers have eaten
sour grapes, and the children's teeth are set on
edge?" As I live, saith the Lord God, ye shall not
have occasion any more to use this proverb in
Israel. . . The son shall not bear the iniquity
of the father, neither shall the father bear the
iniquity of the son; the righteousness of the
righteous shall be upon him, and the wickedness
of the wicked shall be upon him.' And you know,
too, the story from Matthew: 'As Jesus sat at
meat, many publicans and sinners came and sat
down with him and his disciples. And when the
Pharisees saw it, they said unto his disciples,

Why eateth your Master with publicans and sinners?' And from Luke we have the touching story of the tax-collector Zaccheus who climbed a tree his Lord to see. 'And . . . Jesus . . . said unto him . . . come down, for to day I must abide at thy house . . . And when they saw it [it is the Pharisees again], they all murmured, saying, That he was gone to be guest with a man that is a sinner.'

The Pharisees have perhaps always been with us, in one guise or another, and always busy dividing the world between the saved and the sinners, and carefully putting themselves into the first category. But it has remained for our generation in America to adopt their attitude as official policy, to regard it not with the distaste that Matthew and Luke felt for it, but with approval.

The principle of guilt by association was formulated and applied by the notorious A. Mitchell Palmer, so largely responsible for the Red hysteria that came after World War I [1]; it was written into the syndicalist laws of some states; and it even obtained a sort of judicial countenance in that unhappy *Whitney* v. *California* decision which is remembered today only because it furnished the opportunity for one of Justice Brandeis' most eloquent protests against official intolerance.[2] But not until the miscalled Alien Registration Act of 1940 did guilt by association achieve the status of federal law and policy. It became not only a crime but a disability and a sin by virtue of President Truman's Loyalty Order of 22 March 1947 — an order which set up as one standard for employment and dismissal 'membership in, association with, or sympathetic affiliation with any . . . organization, movement, group or combination of persons, designated by the Attorney General as . . . subversive.'[3] Since then this cloud, originally no bigger than a man's hand, has grown until it fills and darkens the whole horizon. For the notion that one might catch the contagion of subversion by 'sympathetic affiliation' with whatever organization some official might think subversive, was clearly the most hospitable and inclusive of catch-alls, and was quickly seized upon by professional patrioteers for partisan and private purposes.

Soon not only the Attorney General of the United States but almost everybody else was busy compiling lists — members of Congressional

committees, state legislative committees, state
attorney generals, and scores of private organizations as well. The lists themselves, needless to
say, grew longer and longer, for increasingly their
compilers followed the principle implicit in
Benjamin Franklin's story of the two Quaker
sisters: 'I know not how it is, sister, but the older
I get the more I find that no one is right but me
and thee, and sometimes I am troubled about
thee.' The list of the House Committee on Un-
American Activities now includes some seven
hundred names. And as the lists grow longer,
the standard of 'affiliation' grows vaguer.[4] To the
witch-hunters of our time no more plausible test
was ever devised than this one, for sooner or
later almost every man or woman who is active
in public affairs joins some organization that
somebody considers subversive. And the shibboleths that 'birds of a feather flock together,'
that 'there is no smoke without fire,' that 'a man
is known by the company he keeps,' are so
widely held that they affect the judgment of
even the most level-headed. Whatever its legal
status, in one sense the doctrine of guilt by
association has already scored a signal triumph,
for by now the most courageous are reluctant to

sign a petition or to join an organization for the most laudable purposes, while the timid simply refuse to sign or to join anything at all.

Yet no more pernicious doctrine has ever found its way into American law or into popular acceptance than this doctrine of guilt by association. It is pernicious in principle, in application, and in consequences. It is based on fear and suspicion, on ignorance and bigotry, on arrogance and vanity. It is designed not to save us or to strengthen us, but to subvert vital parts of our democracy and of our constitutional system.

It is essential, then, that we examine this doctrine critically in order that we may ascertain what it has cost us and understand what it may yet cost us. And when we do this we must avoid, if we can, the natural temptation to reject the doctrine merely because of its ineradicable vulgarity — its mean appeal to vanity and its shabby appeal to prudence and its abject appeal to fear — and consider it rather in terms of its impact and its consequences. Yet though the decisive argument against the doctrine is drawn from history and experience, from an appreciation of the role which voluntary associations have played in our history and of their function in our democratic system, it is not only legitimate but essential that we weigh the logical, the legal, the moral objections to this odious doctrine.

First, then, the doctrine of guilt by association is unsound in logic, and this for a variety of reasons. It is unsound because it assumes that a good cause becomes bad if supported by bad men; perhaps it assumes the reverse, as well — as it logically should — that a bad cause becomes good if supported by virtuous men. But truth stands on its own merits; it may be more acceptable with proper sponsorship, but it is neither enhanced nor impaired by the authorities who support it. It does not run a fever chart of credibility or incredibility as various types of support are proffered to it. If a cause is worthy of support, it does not cease to merit support because men we disapprove support it: if all the subversives in the land asserted that two and two make four, two and two would still make four. This is the principle of science, and this is the principle, too, of Natural Law and Natural Rights.

There is a persuasive reason why conservatives and liberals alike should subscribe to this principle, and that is a practical one. For if bad support could damage a good cause, then all that would be needed to tarnish the Declaration of Independence or to destroy the Constitution would be the endorsement of these documents by the Communist party; all that would be needed to ruin the Republican party or the American Legion or the American Bar Association would be approval of their policies and objectives by the *Daily Worker*. It is a common device — perhaps trick is the better word — of members of Congressional committees to confront witnesses whom they wish to embarrass with the fact that they have been favorably quoted in the *Daily Worker*.[5] But it is well to remember that Herbert Hoover and the late Senator Taft have been cited both frequently and favorably in *Pravda*. The doctrine that a good cause can be damaged by disreputable support is one that cuts both ways.

Second, the doctrine is wrong legally. In Anglo-American law, guilt is personal, not collective. It does not spread, by a process of osmosis, from the guilty to the neighboring innocent. Guilt attaches itself to illegal acts, not to dangerous thoughts or suspicious associations. There is, of course, such a thing as collective guilt in a conspiracy, but conspiracy concerns itself with illegal acts,[6] and laws now on the statute books are ample to take care of these. It is a far cry from joining the World Federalists or the Civil Liberties Union to engaging in conspiracy, and a climate of opinion that befogs the distinction is one in which the most fundamental rights can be lost. The Supreme Court itself has repeatedly repudiated the notion of guilt by association,[7] and it has repudiated, too, the notion that any one man can decide which organizations are legal and which are illegal.[8] Furthermore in our constitutional system, guilt is not retroactive, and the Constitution specifically prohibits the Congress from passing a bill of attainder or an ex post facto law. 'An ex post facto law,' the Supreme Court has said, 'is one which renders an act punishable in a manner in which it was not punishable when it was committed.' It would be difficult to find a more succinct description of the practices in which our Congressional and state legislative investigating committees are now engaged. Thus, for example, Senator McCarthy charged that Dorothy Kenyon had 'been affiliated with at least 28 Communist-front organizations, all of which have been declared subversive by an official Government agency,' but the evidence revealed that of the 20 — not 28 — organizations cited to prove this charge, Miss Kenyon was connected with but one after it was cited as subversive — and that even this citation had not been constitutionally sustained! To punish, either by law or by destruction of character or forfeiture of job, the joining an organization in 1937 or in 1945 which was not held to be subversive until 1950 or later, is a violation of the spirit if not of the letter of the Constitution.[9] More, it is a practice that revolts anyone familiar with the history and traditions of Anglo-American justice.

Third, the doctrine is wrong practically, and this for a variety of reasons. It is wrong practically because when we try to apply it as a yardstick it changes on us like Alice's Cheshire cat and disappears, all but a sardonic grin. To be sure the Attorney General obliges with one list of subversive organizations, the Congressional Committee on Un-American Activities with another, and various state committees, of which the notorious Tenney in California is the most energetic, with still others. But for the most part, federal and state laws and regulations take refuge in a woolly

vagueness: thus the memorable Illinois statute
of 1941 which excluded from the ballot 'groups
associated directly or indirectly with un-American principles' or engaged in propaganda designed to teach subservience to the 'ideals of
foreign nations'; whether the authors had in
mind such foreign doctrines as Manchester
liberalism or *laissez faire* we are not told. Thus
Texas has outlawed groups whose 'principles
include any thought or purpose of setting aside
representative government'; whether this has
reference to the thinking of the Democratic party
about the representation of Negroes we are not
told. Georgia disqualifies for public employment any who have lent the Communist party
'aid, support, advice, counsel or influence';
whether this includes unfriendly advice as well
as friendly we are not told.[10] President Truman's
original Loyalty Order, as we have seen, suffered
from this same ineradicable defect of vagueness,
for what, after all, is 'sympathetic affiliation' with
an 'organization, association, movement, group,
or combination'? So, too, does Attorney General
Brownell's drive on 'security risks,' which lumps
together in one indiscriminate mass every civil
servant dismissed or allowed to resign for almost

any reason. For woolly imprecision it would be hard to match Mr. Brownell's statement in Texas, in December 1953, that the government had been cleaned out of all persons 'suspected of Communist tendencies.' Suspected by whom? and what are 'Communist tendencies'? This is as if a sheriff should announce that he had taken away the driving licenses of all persons suspected of a tendency to drive recklessly!

But even if it were possible to import some concreteness and clarity into the definition of subversive organizations, it would still be neither possible nor desirable for our people to engage in a check of membership, past as well as present, of all organizations to which we belong or which we are asked to join. What a shambles our society would be if we actually did this. We should be careful what we join, we are told; we should be careful in lending our name, or our countenance. But how do we go about being careful? Do we start with our church, our labor union, our fraternal society, our veterans' organization, our professional group? Do we investigate the membership lists of all the organizations to which we belong, or which we propose to join, and how do we go about discovering the character of a

thousand or a hundred thousand members? If
the presence of 'subversives' in an organization
is enough to persuade us to drop our membership, all the Communists need to do to destroy
any society — say the Republican party or the
American Legion or the Methodist Church — is
to join it. Do we wish to encourage this? Or
should we perhaps do what a good many organizations are now doing — require loyalty oaths,
appoint committees to investigate membership,
and purge our organizations of undesirables?
That organizations must rid themselves of
trouble-makers is clear, and neither the principle
nor the practice is new. This is a very different
thing from challenging and testing the faithful-
ness and loyalty of their members. A better way
than this to introduce confusion and discord into
organizations could not be devised. If the Communists can force or maneuver us into such misguided practices, they will have won a notable
victory.

It is relevant to note, too, in connection with
the impracticality of the enforcement of the
principle of guilt by association, that the principle, as it operates, is actually more one of chain
reaction than of association. Those familiar with

our history will recall that this was true a century and a half ago when Jefferson's intellectual 'affiliations' with the Enlightenment and the French Revolution exposed him to the memorable charge from President Timothy Dwight of Yale College that his triumph would mean that 'our churches . . . become temples of reason . . . our psalms of praise Marseillaise hymns . . . our wives and daughters, the victims of legal prostitution . . . our sons disciples of Voltaire and the dragoons of Marat.' [11] Half a century later the same chain-reaction theory was used against the abolitionists. 'Whenever you found an abolitionist,' said a Boston newspaper — Boston, mind you — 'you found an anti-hanging man, woman's rights man, an infidel . . . a socialist, a red republican, a fanatical teetotaler, a believer in mesmerism and Rochester rappings.' And the *Richmond Enquirer* wrote in 1856 that the slogan of the Republican party — the Republican, mind you — ought to be 'free niggers, free women, free land, free love, and Frémont.' [12] How this chain reaction works today is clear to anyone who follows the labyrinthine arguments and conclusions of the House Un-American Activities Committee in relation to such an organi-

zation as the Southern Conference for Human
Welfare,[13] or of the Tenney Committee in regard
to the Civil Liberties Union.[14]

Perhaps the most curious thing about this
principle of collective contamination is its selective character. It operates, clearly, on a double
standard, but who sets the standard, and how, is
impenetrably obscure. No one suggests the
danger of association with the Daughters of the
American Revolution, or the American Legion,
or the Democratic party, yet it is entirely possible
to make out a case against each of these organizations — a case quite as plausible as that made
out against the Civil Liberties Union, for example — for at one time or another each of these
organizations has been guilty of un-American intolerance, or of encouraging and conniving at the
violation of the First and the Fourteenth Amend-
ments. And, after all, if Republicans can associate with a McCarthy and Democrats with a
McCarran without ostensible infection, it is
difficult to know where we are to draw the line or
establish our moral quarantine.

There are, needless to say, dangers in promis-
cuous joining or name-lending. But we must
leave something to the individual judgment,

something to common sense, something to the natural law of diminishing returns. Those who join organizations without proper inquiry into their purpose or direction, or who lend their names indiscriminately to causes and organizations, will soon discover that they are tagged as 'joiners,' that they suffer embarrassment and confusion, and that they forfeit much of the influence they once commanded. It is scarcely necessary for government to concern itself with excessive joining or signing, any more than it concerns itself with unwillingness to join or to sign.[15]

Even the majority report of the subcommittee exonerating Judge Dorothy Kenyon from the charge of subversive affiliations, for example, goes out of its way to rebuke her for joining so many organizations without prudent investigation and discrimination. 'The evidence before this subcommittee,' reads the report, 'makes it apparent that she was less than judicious in joining certain organizations during the late 1930's and the early 1940's.' The impropriety of this should be apparent. If individual members of the committee wished to express their individual opinions on this matter, they were of course entitled to do so, and doubtless Judge Kenyon, and her associates, would accord these opinions the respect they deserved. But what business has an official body in our government expressing official opinions on this matter? Government has no more right to decide — or even to comment on — how many organizations we join than it has to decide or comment on how many churches or fraternal societies we join. Except where conspiracy is involved, these things must be left to the discretion of the individual.

Certainly no one should give his name to an organization gratuitously, without some investigation or assurance of its character. But clearly there are practical difficulties here, for we cannot spend all of our time investigating each organization that appeals to us for support, nor do we want an official body to make the investigations and the decisions for us. On the whole if we must err — as we will — it is probably better for society that we err on the side of generosity and faith than on the side of caution and fear. And we must beware, too, lest we erect a double standard in this matter of lending our names and our support to causes and organizations. It ill becomes a society that applauds the stars of the film, television, radio, and sports world when they lend their names — for a price — to the endorsement of breakfast food they do not eat, soap they do not use, whiskey they do not drink — to become indignant when misguided idealists lend their names to what they think are worthy causes. They may be mistaken, but surely an excess of enthusiasm and hope is better than deception and hypocrisy.

A more serious problem arises in the divorce, or gap, between membership and responsibility. On the whole it is certainly desirable that those who join an organization take part in its activities and assume some share of responsibility for its direction. If its character is not what it purports to be, if its activities are not those the members originally supported, then they should either work to change it or, if they are unable to do this or do not care enough to try, they should get out. If they fail to do either they may expect to be charged with irresponsibility.

Here again, however, we must beware of a double standard. When our whole society operates to divorce membership from responsibility it is not fair to require that liberals and reformers be different from the rest of us. After all, all

those who own shares in a corporation — and
there are millions of them — own the corporation and are ultimately responsible for its conduct. Yet how many shareholders pay any attention whatever to the character or conduct of the
corporations they partially own except to watch
the dividend reports? How many shareholders
interest themselves in the labor policies or the
taxation policies or the conservation policies of
their corporations? [16] For that matter, how many
of those who insist — and quite rightly too — that
those who join organizations should take an
active part in them, themselves take an active
part in the political party to which they belong,
in the affairs of their church, their fraternal
organization, their professional societies? If we
applied to the average person, who belongs after
all to a good many organizations, the tests we
are now asked to apply to such public figures as
Bishop Oxnam or Mildred McAfee Horton or
Judge Kenyon, a great many of our parties,
churches, and professional organizations would
collapse overnight.

Fourth, the doctrine of guilt by association is
wrong historically, for it flies in the face of our
experience and of the experience of the English-

speaking peoples. If there is one thing that has always distinguished the English, and the American, peoples, it is their faith in voluntary associations as the way to get things done. Reliance on voluntary associations is a habit that goes back for several hundred years — back to the days of the joint-stock company and the Congregational Church. Where France and Spain used agencies of the royal government to conquer and settle and rule their overseas empires, the English were using the joint-stock company — the Massachusetts Bay Company or the Virginia Company, for example — or they were permitting religious congregations (private associations) to undertake the great task of colonization. The habit so deeply ingrained in our history persisted and flourished, until the voluntary association became perhaps the most characteristic of all American social institutions.

So Tocqueville thought when he made his magisterial survey of the United States in the 1830's.

'In no country in the world [he wrote] has the principle of association been more successfully used, or more unsparingly applied to a multitude of different objects, than in America. . . The citizen of the United States is taught from his

earliest infancy to rely upon his own exertions, in
order to resist the evils and difficulties of life. . .
Wherever at the head of some new undertaking
you see the Government in France, or a man of
rank in England, in the United States you will be
sure to find an association.' [17]

And again, with even greater relevance:

'Nothing is more deserving of our attention than
the intellectual and moral associations of America. The political and industrial associations of
that country strike us forcibly; but the others
elude our observation, or if we discover them,
we understand them imperfectly, because we
have hardly ever seen anything of the kind. It
must however be acknowledged that they are as
necessary to the American people as the former,
and perhaps more so. In democratic countries
the science of association is the mother of science;
the progress of all the rest depends upon the
progress it has made.' [18]

No one familiar with American history can
doubt that the private voluntary association is
the most basic of American institutions, for it
is the institution that underlies almost all others.
America was settled largely by voluntary associations; the early New England governments —
and to some extent those elsewhere — were the

creations of such organizations; and when it came time to set up as an independent nation, Americans seized upon the instrument of the voluntary association: the first government of the thirteen colonies was called The Association, and it was just that.

Our churches are all private voluntary associations, and have been ever since the Revolution and its aftermath broke the connection between church and state. Our political parties are private voluntary associations, unknown even to the law until recent years. Our labor unions, fraternal orders, clubs, business and professional societies — the bar associations and medical associations and chambers of commerce, the associations of scholars and of librarians, of artists and musicians, of alumni and of veterans — all are voluntary. Most of our colleges and universities are the products of such voluntary associations.

Most of our reforms, too, have been carried through by just such organizations — many of them regarded as disreputable or subversive by States its most distinctive character over the past their respectable contemporaries. Call the list of those reforms that have given the United States its most distinctive character over the past

century and a half and you will discover that
almost all of them had their inception in, and
were carried to completion by, associations of
individuals. Thus the abolition of slavery, tem-
perance, women's rights, prison and penal reforms, educational reform, slum clearance, the
peace movement, the protection of Indians, of
Negroes, of the foreign-born from exploitation
— these and a hundred others belong in this
category.

But it is needless to elaborate on anything so
obvious. We are a nation of joiners,[19] and it is by
joining that we get most of the business of
democracy done. We have not yet learned to
turn automatically to the Government to do
what we want, though the McCarthys and the
Veldes and the Jenners may yet persuade us that
we have to do this. For it is, of course, these men
who extol private enterprise in the economic
realm who are the mortal enemies of private
enterprise in the spiritual and the intellectual
realms. And it is only here that the issue is important, for if you stifle private enterprise in the
intellectual realm you stifle it everywhere. It is
these men who are so alarmed at Big Government, and who campaign against it so heatedly

when it appears as the TVA, for example, or as federal aid to education, who are in fact the architects of Big Government. For a government that has to do what private organizations have heretofore done will indeed be big. And a government that may decide which organizations are safe and which are unsafe will be strong enough to impose its ideas and principles on everyone. Again the warning of Tocqueville is timely:

'If once the sovereign had a general right of authorizing associations of all kinds upon certain conditions, he would not be long without claiming the right of superintending and managing them, in order to prevent them from departing from the rules laid down by himself. In this manner, the State, after having reduced all who are desirous of forming associations into dependence, would proceed to reduce into the same condition all who belong to associations already formed — that is to say, almost all the men who are now in existence.' [20]

There is a very special reason why Americans have always been so zealous to do business through private enterprise, why they seem more zealous here than even the British. For the private association here has played a decisive role not only in democracy but in nationalism as well. Here, in the United States, it has operated in two ways, unconsciously of course, but massively. In the first place it has broken down the organizations of actual government into a thousand, a hundred thousand, manageable parts. Doubtless we must have state school systems, but in fact each community, big or little, runs its own schools through its local school boards, even through Parent Teachers Associations. Doubtless we must have state regulation of our professional standards and conduct, but in fact the local bar or medical associations pretty much determine standards and practices, and each community runs its own hospital — perhaps a dozen organizations co-operating in the work. In scores of ways the private organization has functioned to make the giant task of government more manageable, more understandable, and even familiar on the local level. In a country as large as the United States, where the national government might so easily become a Leviathan, this fragmentation and decentralization is of utmost importance.

But at the same time the private organization has had an effect which, at first sight, may appear to be just the opposite of this. It has had a nationalizing effect. It has cut athwart local and state boundaries, tying together people of various states, sections, classes, and interests. The Connecticut doctor is allied with the California doctor, the Vermont hunter with the Minnesota hunter, the stamp collector in Massachusetts with the stamp collector in Florida; the Rotary in Hartford, the chapter of Kappa Sigma at Cornell, the Chamber of Commerce of Cincinnati, the Knights of Columbus at Boston are all connected with their opposite numbers in every state of the Union, and all help to form a network of association and interest that binds the Union itself together. In a nation as big as all of western Europe, and as easily fragmented by nature, economic interests, and religious differences, this function of the private voluntary association has been, and continues to be, of capital importance.

Now if we strike at the principle and the practice of voluntary association, we strike at all this tradition and practice which forms so large a part of our history. We endanger the working machinery of democracy. We endanger the working machinery of nationalism. We endanger the working machinery of equalitarianism, of the

classless society. We open wide the gates to the
entry of Big Government, or to the control of
those social, intellectual, and moral activities that
have always been thought to be private or local
in character, and which have flourished best
when kept private and local.

For we must look to the logical consequences
of whatever principles we accept and whatever
course of conduct we adopt. The logical consequence of the doctrine of guilt by association is
that men will cease to join new organizations
and will drop away from old ones — for you never
know which ones may be infected. Already ordinary men and women are timid about joining —
and who can blame them? Already college students refrain from political or reform activities —
and who can blame them? Nor need we delude
ourselves that it is only the lunatic fringe, the
expendable organizations that will suffer. We
are all of us members of many societies, and
when the principle of association is attacked, we
may say with John Donne, ask not for whom the
bell tolls, it tolls for all of us. Already the
Unitarian Church is suspect in some quarters;
elsewhere it is the Civil Liberties Union, or the
World Federalists, or the friends of UNESCO,

or the American Library Association which has so courageously fought book censorship, or the Society of Friends whose advocacy of peace disturbs some super-patriots, or perhaps the entire teaching profession. In time it may be one of the major churches or a major party, for a Committee that can hire a man who suspects the Protestant clergy of harboring seven thousand Communists and fellow-travelers is capable of anything.

Once the notion that joining may be dangerous is firmly established, all of our organizations will be affected, and all of our institutions of government, of education, of science, of the arts. Then American democracy will dry up at the roots. That this process is already under way and already taking its toll is clear from the findings of Jahoda and Cook in their study of 'Security Measures and Freedom of Thought' in the federal civil service.

'One of the consequences of the loyalty and security programs [they tell us] has been the development of a social atmosphere in which individuals are subject to unfounded suspicion on the basis of certain personal characteristics or group memberships. . . We asked all Federal employes interviewed in Washington what kinds of people they thought might form the target for unfounded suspicion. . . Among the list [of answers] one group may be singled out for comment because of the frequency with which it is named by respondents of very different outlook . . . The group we have in mind are the people who belong to voluntary organizations with definite social purposes. . . At present voluntary organizations are not proscribed in this country. Yet our material suggests the possibility that because membership in some organizations can have dire consequences, for Federal employes, "a public opinion passes current which tends to cause any association whatsoever to be regarded as a bold and almost an illicit enterprise." ' [21]

Thus the present-day wrecking crew may wreck one of the props of our democratic and our constitutional system. And while they are about this, they are engaged in a related and equally subversive activity. That is the attack upon the right of petition, a right so important that it occupies an honored place in both the English and the American Revolutions. The right of petition is not openly attacked, to be sure; even the McCarthys are not quite that impudent. But the attack upon it is no less deadly for that. After all, if petitioning for clemency for the Rosenbergs, for example, or for the abolition of the Un-American Activities Committee, is to expose men and women to the charge of subversion, to the nuisance and expense of investigation, to loss of passport perhaps — they will think twice before signing anything. Some time ago a Wisconsin newspaper sent out reporters to get signatures to the preamble of the Declaration of Independence. Out of 112 persons asked to sign, only one was prepared to do so; the others regarded the document as subversive or dangerous — which of course it is. And it was not long ago that one remorseful Hollywood star avowed that hereafter he would never sign anything except on the advice of at least three lawyers. If only George III could have inculcated that attitude of mind in the Americans of 1776 there would never have been any nonsense about signing a Declaration of Independence.

Finally the doctrine of guilt by association is wrong morally. It is wrong morally because it assumes a far greater power in evil than in virtue. It is based therefore on a desperate view of mankind. It rests on what may be called the rotten-apple theory of society — the theory that one wicked man corrupts all virtuous men, and that

one mistaken idea subverts all sound ideas. This
business of contamination, be it noted, works
only one way. Apparently one Communist or one
subversive can contaminate an entire organization, but a thousand Republicans or Legion-
naires are without perceptible influence!

Why is there no doctrine of innocence by association? Why is it that our present-day grave-
diggers pay this frightened tribute to the power
of communism, that they think its doctrines ir-
resistible? Why is it that they tremble for the
fate of twenty thousand students if they find two
or three Communists or ex-Communists on a
faculty, but take no apparent satisfaction in
the presence of one or two thousand loyal men
and women? Why is it that they fear for an entire
community if they find the works of Karl Marx
or perhaps of Henry Wallace or Howard Fast on
its library shelves, but take no reassurance from
the presence there of thousands of volumes from
the pens of the great host of the free?

It is, of course, because they are men consumed
with fear and hatred, they are men who know
nothing of the stirring history of freedom, they
are men of little faith. We may go further and
say that they are hypocrites in that they do not

even believe in the doctrines that they so loudly proclaim. For if they did sincerely believe them, they would not fear counter-argument, but would be willing to submit their own beliefs to the competition of the market place of ideas. Suppression and intimidation are, after all, confessions of fear and of guilt.

The doctrine of guilt by association is wrong morally for other reasons as well. It is wrong because it caters to spiritual pride and puts a premium on arrogance and vanity. It assumes that it is possible to divide mankind into the saved and the sinners (or, if you will, the loyal and the disloyal, the patriotic and the subversive, the American and the un-American), and that the saved must never associate with the sinners.

Who are these men to whom all truth is revealed, yea even the knowledge of the saved and the damned? Who are they that know so surely which causes are good and which are bad, which motives are noble and which are ignoble? They are very sure of themselves, these self-appointed guardians of our loyalty and our patriotism and our morality. They are sure that whosoever else may go astray and support the wrong causes, they never go astray, they support only respectable causes; that whosoever else may read dangerous books, they read only pure books; that whosoever else may sign misguided petitions, they never sign anything that they should not sign; that whosoever else is un-American, they are truly American; that whosoever else is disloyal, they are loyal. 'Let us judge not that we be not judged,' said Lincoln of the slave-holders, but our current Pharisees are ready to judge everything and everybody.

There is one consolation here, and that is that the society of the saved gets more and more exclusive and the society of the damned larger and larger. Just as each new party that came to power during the French Revolution thought it essential to send its predecessors to the guillotine for lack of true zeal, so the hate-mongers of our day are spreading their nets wider and wider until in the end hardly anyone can escape. Not the former head of the WAVES, for example, for she supported too many international causes; not Secretary of State Dulles, for he associated — even sympathetically — with Alger Hiss; not General Marshall, for he sold out to the Chinese Communists; not Mrs. Roosevelt, for she has sponsored a hundred suspicious reforms, and actually served in the United Nations; not former President Truman, for he knowingly appointed spies to high office; not President Eisenhower, for he associated with Soviet Russia during the war and is an internationalist to boot. The whole performance reminds one of the antics of those religious fanatics who indulge in schism after schism, consigning those who differ from them on nice points of theology to eternal damnation.

The doctrine of guilt by association, then, is deeply immoral. It rests on a low view of human nature. It panders to spiritual pride and arrogance. It confesses a lack of faith in truth and in virtue. It dries up all our decent and generous instincts. It makes us into those odious men and women who are ever conscious of their own rectitude and puffed up with their own importance, and who are very careful never to expose themselves to the risks of battle or of life — men and women who never support any but the most respectable causes, read any but the approved books, associate with any but respectable people. It is relevant to remember that in the beginning and for a longer time than the United States has existed, Christianity was disreputable and Christians contemptible. And when we are tempted —

as at times all of us are — to look askance at some of the enthusiasts who are so zealous in good causes, it is well to remember what the Reverend Samuel J. May — uncle to the Little Women — said a century ago of the Abolitionists: 'We Abolitionists are what we are — babes, sucklings, obscure men, silly women, publicans and sinners, and we shall manage this matter just as might be expected of such persons as we are. It is unbecoming in abler men who stood by and would do nothing, to complain because we do not do better.'

It is time that we see this doctrine of guilt by association for what it is: not a useful device for detecting subversion, but a device for subverting our constitutional principles and practices, for destroying our constitutional guarantees, and for corrupting our faith in ourselves and in our fellow men.

NOTES

1. This story is dispassionately set forth in Z. Chafee, *Free Speech in the United States.*

2. 'Those who won our independence believed that the final end of the state was to make men

free to develop their faculties; and that in its
government the deliberative forces should prevail over the arbitrary. They valued liberty both
as an end and as a means. They believed liberty
to be the secret of happiness and courage the secret of liberty. They believed that freedom to
think as you will and to speak as you think are
means indispensable to the discovery and spread
of political truth; that without free speech and
assembly discussion would be futile; that with
them, discussion affords ordinarily adequate protection against the dissemination of noxious doctrine; that the greatest menace to freedom is an
inert people; that public discussion is a political
duty; and that this should be a fundamental principle of American government. They recognized
the risks to which all human institutions are subject. But they knew that order cannot be secured
merely through fear of punishment for its infrac-
tion; that it is hazardous to discourage thought,
hope, and imagination; that fear breeds repression; that repression breeds hate; that hate men-
aces stable government; that the path of safety
lies in the opportunity to discuss freely supposed
grievances and proposed remedies; and that the
fitting remedy for evil counsels is good ones. Be-
lieving in the power of reason as applied through
public discussion, they eschewed silence coerced
by law — the argument of force in its worst form.
Recognizing the occasional tyrannies of govern-

ment majorities, they amended the Constitution so that free speech and assembly should be guaranteed.' *Whitney* v. *California* (274 U.S. 357 at 375).

3. The text can be found in my *Documents of American History,* Doc. 579. And see my comment on the Order, 'Washington Witch-hunt,' *The Nation,* 5 April 1947.

4. Thus Edward L. Barrett in his *The Tenney Committee:* 'Individuals were found [by the Committee] to be communist sympathizers because they belonged to a number of organizations termed "communist fronts." And the organizations were found to be communist fronts because the individuals were connected with them. Such circular reasoning created an ever-increasing group of individuals who could be listed because of their membership in organizations and an ever-increasing group of organizations which would be listed because these individuals belonged to them' (p. 350).

5. Thus, in his radio reply to former President Truman in November 1953, Senator McCarthy sought to confound Truman by asserting that Truman's criticism of him was taken 'word for word' from the *Daily Worker.* And thus, too, one of the many reasons why Mr. Fulton Lewis, Jr., disapproved of this article when it appeared in *The New York Times* was that it was quoted with approval by the *Daily Worker.*

6. See *Dennis* v. *United States* (341 U.S. 494). As Justice Jackson said, 'What is really under review here is a conviction of conspiracy, after a trial for conspiracy, on an indictment charging conspiracy, brought under a statute outlawing conspiracy.' The confusion of 'guilt by association' with 'conspiracy' is widespread and dangerous. See in this connection John Lord O'Brian, 'Loyalty Tests and Guilt by Association,' 61 *Harvard Law Review* 592, and 'Guilt by Association — Three Words in Search of a Meaning,' 17 *U. of Chicago Law Review* 148.

7. Thus in *De Jonge* v. *Oregon* (299 U.S. 353) the Court in voiding an indictment against De Jonge for attending a Communist meeting held 'If the persons assemblying have committed crimes elsewhere, if they have formed or are engaged in a conspiracy against the public peace and order, they may be prosecuted for their conspiracy or other violations of valid laws. But it is a different matter when the State, instead of prosecuting them for such offenses, seizes upon mere participation in a peaceable assembly and a lawful public discussion as the basis for a criminal charge.' Thus in the Schneiderman case (320 U.S. 118) the Court said, 'It is appropriate to mention that under our traditions beliefs are personal and not a matter of mere association, and that men in adhering to a political party or other organization do not subscribe

unqualifiedly to all of its platforms or asserted principles.'

Thus in *Bridges* v. *Wixon* (326 U.S. 125) Justice Murphy said that 'the doctrine of personal guilt is one of the most fundamental principles of our jurisprudence. It partakes of the very essence of the concept of freedom and due process of law. It prevents the persecution of the innocent for the beliefs and actions of others.' Thus in *Wieman* v. *Updegraff* (344 U.S. 183) the Court, nullifying an Oklahoma act requiring state and public employees to take an oath that they are not and for five years have not been affiliated with any organization listed by the Attorney General of the U.S. as subversive, said, 'Membership may be innocent. . . At the time of affiliation, a group itself may be innocent, only later coming under the influence of those who would turn it towards illegitimate ends. Conversely an organization formerly subversive and therefore designated as such may have subsequently freed itself from the influences which originally led to its listing.'

The decision of a divided Court in *Adler et al.* v. *Bd. of Education of N. Y.* (342 U.S. 485) suggests that the Court will be reluctant to intervene where the issue is not so much one of 'guilt' as of the right to teach in the public schools, on the basis of associations. Judge Minton said: 'One's associates, past and present, as well as one's conduct, may properly be considered in determining fitness and loyalty. . . In the employment of officials and teachers of the school system, the state may very properly inquire into the company they keep, and we know of no rule . . . that prevents the State, when determining fitness, and loyalty of such persons, from considering the organizations and persons with whom they associate.' But Judge Minton hastened to qualify these generalizations by adding that the 'association' to which the disqualified person belonged must be 'one that advocated the overthrow of government by unlawful means and that the person employed was a member of the organization and *knew of its purpose*' (ital. mine). In his dissenting opinion Justice Douglas said: 'The present law proceeds on a principle repugnant to our society — guilt by association. . . The mere fact of membership in the organization raises a prima facie case of her [the teacher's] own guilt. She may, it is said, show her innocence, but innocence in this case turns on knowledge; and when the witch hunt is on, one who must rely on ignorance leans on a feeble reed.'

And he added a warning which this essay is designed to emphasize and elaborate: 'Any organization committed to a liberal cause, any group organized to revolt against an hysterical trend, any committee launched to sponsor an unpopular program becomes suspect. These are the

organizations into which Communists often in-
filtrate. Their presence infects the whole, even
though the project was not conceived in sin. A
teacher caught in that mesh is almost certain to
stand condemned. Fearing condemnation she
will tend to shrink from any association that stirs
up controversy. In that manner freedom of expression will be stifled' (ibid. at 509).

8. On this point see Justice Jackson, in *West
Virginia Bd. of Education* v. *Barnette* (319 U.S.
624): 'If there is any fixed star in our constitutional constellation, it is that no official, high or
petty, can prescribe what shall be orthodox in
politics, nationalism, religion, or other matters
of opinion, or force citizens to confess by word
or act their faith therein.'

9. See in this connection *U.S.* v. *Lovett, Watson
and Dodd* (328 U.S. 303).

10. See, for an analysis of this and comparable
legislation, Walter Gellhorn, *The States and Subversion*, and William B. Prendergast, 'State Legislatures and Communism,' 44 *American Political Science Review*, p. 556ff.

11. See C. A. Beard, *Economic Origins of Jeffer-
sonian Democracy*, p. 356.

12. For this and other illuminating quotations,
see Russel B. Nye, *Fettered Freedom*, and Clem-

ent Eaton, *Freedom of Thought in the Old South*.

13. See the careful examination of this in Robert K. Carr, *The House Committee on Un-American Activities*, 1945-1950, especially p. 337ff.

14. See Edward L. Barrett, *The Tenney Committee*, especially ch. 10.

15. State Department Employee Loyalty Investigation, 81 Cong. 2d Sess. Report, no. 2108, p. 47.

16. Note, in this connection, the warning sounded by former Attorney General Francis Biddle: 'The principle of group responsibility is a dangerous one, and is subject to extension in other fields, where it fits as logically as on the domain of loyalty standards. If members of a subversive organization are to be charged with responsibility for its platform or principles . . . the same reasoning applies to other fictitious bodies, alike to corporations and labor unions. Stockholders own the corporation. By this logic they could be made liable criminally for its acts, for the acts of the directors, and indeed, to carry the logic to its ultimate, for the acts of the other stockholders. The argument is less fantastic than it sounds. Complaints have been made, from time to time, that criminal indictments under the Sherman Anti-Trust Act have included corporate officers who on the record had no knowl-

edge of what had been done, on the theory that even if they did not know they should have known and ought to be held responsible' (*The Fear of Freedom*, p. 101).

17. *Democracy in America* (H. S. Commager, ed.), Oxford University Press, 1947, pp. 109, 319.

18. Ibid. p. 323.

19. On this see A. M. Schlesinger, 'A Nation of Joiners' in *Paths to the Present,* 1949.

20. *Democracy in America,* op. cit. p. 484.

21. 61 *Yale Law Journal* 295.

V

Who Is Loyal to America?

On 6 May 1947 a Russian-born girl, Mrs. Shura Lewis, gave a talk to the students of the Western High School of Washington, D.C. She talked about Russia—its school system, its public-health program, the position of women, of the aged, of the workers, the farmers, and the professional classes — and compared, superficially and uncritically, some American and Russian social institutions. The most careful examination of the speech — happily reprinted for us in the *Congressional Record* — does not disclose a single disparagement of anything American unless it is a quasi-humorous reference to the cost of having a baby and of dental treatment in this country. Mrs. Lewis said nothing that had not been said at least a thousand times, in speeches, in newspapers, magazines, and books. She said nothing that any normal person could find objectionable.

Her speech, however, created a sensation. A few students walked out on it. Others improvised placards proclaiming their devotion to Americanism. Indignant mothers telephoned their protests. Newspapers took a strong stand against the outrage. Congress, rarely concerned for the political or economic welfare of the citizens of the capital city, reacted sharply when its intellectual welfare was at stake. Congressmen Rankin and Dirksen thundered and lightninged; the District of Columbia Committee went into a huddle; there were demands for housecleaning in the whole school system, which was obviously shot through and through with communism.

All this might be ignored, for we have learned not to expect either intelligence or understanding of Americanism from this element in our Congress. More ominous was the reaction of the educators entrusted with the high responsibility of guiding and guarding the intellectual welfare of our boys and girls. Did they stand up for intellectual freedom? Did they insist that high-school children have the right and the duty to learn about other countries? Did they protest that students are to be trusted to use intelligence and common sense? Did they affirm that the Americanism of their students is staunch enough to resist propaganda? Did they perform even the elementary task, expected of educators above all, of analyzing the much criticized speech?

Not at all. The District Superintendent of Schools, Dr. Hobart Corning, hastened to agree with the animadversions of Representatives Rankin and Dirksen. The whole thing was, he confessed, 'a very unfortunate occurrence,' and had 'shocked the whole school system.' What Mrs. Lewis said, he added gratuitously, was 'repugnant to all who are working with youth in the Washington schools,' and 'the entire affair contrary to the philosophy of education under which we operate.' Mr. Danowsky, the hapless principal of the Western High School, was 'the most shocked and regretful of all.' The District of Columbia Committee would be happy to know that though he was innocent in the matter, he had been properly reprimanded!

It is the reaction of the educators that makes this episode more than a tempest in a teapot. We expect hysteria from Mr. Rankin and some newspapers; we are shocked when we see educators, timid before criticism and confused about

first principles, betray their trust. And we won-
der what can be that 'philosophy of education'
which believes that young people can be trained
to the duties of citizenship by wrapping their
minds in cotton-wool.

Merely by talking about Russia Mrs. Lewis was
thought to be attacking Americanism. It is in-
dicative of the seriousness of the situation that
during this same week the House found it necessary to take time out from the discussion of the
labor bill, the tax bill, the International Trade
Organization, and the world famine to meet as-
saults upon Americanism from a new quarter.
This time it was the artists who were undermin-
ing the American system, and members of the
House spent some hours passing around repro-
ductions of the paintings which the State Department had sent abroad as part of its program
for advertising American culture. We need not
pause over the exquisite humor which Congressmen displayed in their comments on modern
art: weary statesmen must have their fun. But we
may profitably remark the major criticism which
was directed against this unfortunate collection
of paintings. What was wrong with these paint-

ings, it shortly appeared, was that they were un-
American. 'No American drew those crazy pic-
tures,' said Mr. Rankin — who ought to know.
The copious files of the Committee on Un-American Activities were levied upon to prove that
of the forty-five artists represented 'no less than
twenty were definitely New Deal in various
shades of Communism.' The damning facts are
specified for each of the pernicious twenty; we
can content ourselves with the first of them, Ben-
Zion. What is the evidence here? 'Ben-Zion was
one of the signers of a letter sent to President
Roosevelt by the United American Artists which
urged help to the USSR and Britain after Hitler
attacked Russia.' He was, in short, a fellow-traveler of Churchill and Roosevelt.

The same day that Mr. Dirksen was denouncing the Washington school authorities for allow-
ing students to hear about Russia ('In Russia,'
Mrs. Lewis said, 'equal right is granted to each
nationality. There is no discrimination. Nobody
says, you are a Negro, you are a Jew'), Representative Williams of Mississippi rose to denounce the *Survey-Graphic* magazine and to add
further to our understanding of Americanism.
The *Survey-Graphic,* he said, 'contained 129

pages of outrageously vile and nauseating anti-Southern, anti-Christian, un-American, and pro-Communist tripe, ostensibly directed toward the elimination of the custom of racial segregation in the South.' It was written by 'meddling un-American purveyors of hate and indecency.'

All in all, a busy week for the House. Yet those who make a practice of reading their *Record* will agree that it was a typical week. For increasingly Congress is concerned with the eradication of disloyalty and the defense of Americanism, and scarcely a day passes that some Congressman does not treat us to exhortations and admonitions, impassioned appeals and eloquent declamations, similar to those inspired by Mrs. Lewis, Mr. Ben-Zion, and the editors of the *Survey-Graphic*. And scarcely a day passes that the outlines of the new loyalty and the new Americanism are not etched more sharply in public policy.

And this is what is significant — the emergence of new patterns of Americanism and of loyalty, patterns radically different from those which have long been traditional. It is not only the Congress that is busy designing the new patterns. They are outlined in President Truman's Loyalty Order of March 1947; in similar orders formu-

lated by the New York City Council and by state
and local authorities throughout the country; in
the programs of the Daughters of the American
Revolution, the American Legion, and similar
patriotic organizations; in the editorials of the
Hearst and the McCormick-Patterson papers;
and in an elaborate series of advertisements sponsored by large corporations and business organizations. In the making is a revival of the Red
hysteria of the early 1920's, one of the shabbiest
chapters in the history of American democracy;
and more than a revival, for the new crusade is
designed not merely to frustrate communism but
to formulate a positive definition of Americanism, and a positive concept of loyalty.

* * * *

What is the new loyalty? It is, above all, conformity. It is the uncritical and unquestioning
acceptance of America as it is — the political institutions, the social relationships, the economic
practices. It rejects inquiry into the race question or socialized medicine, or public housing,
or into the wisdom or validity of our foreign
policy. It regards as particularly heinous any
challenge to what is called 'the system of private

enterprise,' identifying that system with Americanism. It abandons evolution, repudiates the once popular concept of progress, and regards America as a finished product, perfect and complete.

It is, it must be added, easily satisfied. For it wants not intellectual conviction or spiritual conquest but mere outward conformity. In matters of loyalty it takes the word for the deed, the gesture for the principle. It is content with the flag salute, and does not pause to consider the warning of our Supreme Court that 'a person gets from a symbol the meaning he puts into it, and what is one man's comfort and inspiration is another's jest and scorn.' It is satisfied with membership in respectable organizations and, as it assumes that every member of a liberal organization is a Communist, concludes that every member of a conservative one is a true American. It has not yet learned that not everyone who saith Lord, Lord, shall enter into the kingdom of Heaven. It is designed neither to discover real disloyalty nor to foster true loyalty.

What is wrong with this new concept of loyalty? What, fundamentally, is wrong with the pusillanimous retreat of the Washington educators, the antics of Washington legislators, the outcries of alarm from the American Legion, the vulgar appeals of business corporations? It is not merely that these things are offensive. It is rather that they are wrong — morally, socially, and politically.

The concept of loyalty as conformity is a false one. It is narrow and restrictive, denies freedom of thought and of conscience, and is irremediably stained by private and selfish considerations. 'Enlightened loyalty,' wrote Josiah Royce, who made loyalty the very core of his philosophy,

'means harm to no man's loyalty. It is at war only with disloyalty, and its warfare, unless necessity constrains, is only a spiritual warfare. It does not foster class hatreds; it knows of nothing reasonable about race prejudices; and it regards all races of men as one in their need of loyalty. It ignores mutual misunderstandings. It loves its own wherever upon earth its own, namely loyalty itself, is to be found.'

Justice, charity, wisdom, spirituality, he added, were all definable in terms of loyalty, and we may properly ask which of these qualities our contemporary champions of loyalty display.

Above all, loyalty must be to something larger than oneself, untainted by private purposes or selfish ends. But what are we to say of the attempts by the NAM and by individual corporations to identify loyalty with the system of private enterprise? Is it not as if officeholders should attempt to identify loyalty with their own party, their own political careers? Do not those corporations which pay for full-page advertisements associating Americanism with the competitive system expect, ultimately, to profit from that association? Do not those organizations that deplore, in the name of patriotism, the extension of government operation of hydro-electric power expect to profit from their campaign?

Certainly it is a gross perversion not only of the concept of loyalty but of the concept of Americanism to identify it with a particular economic system. This precise question, interestingly enough, came before the Supreme Court in the Schneiderman case of 1943 — and it was Wendell Willkie who was counsel for Schneiderman. Said the Court:

'Throughout our history many sincere people whose attachment to the general Constitutional scheme cannot be doubted have, for various and even divergent reasons, urged differing degrees of governmental ownership and control of natural resources, basic means of production, and banks and the media of exchange, either with or without compensation. And something once regarded as a species of private property was abolished without compensating the owners when the institution of slavery was forbidden. Can it be said that the author of the Emancipation Proclamation and the supporters of the Thirteenth Amendment were not attached to the Constitution?'

There is, it should be added, a further danger in the willful identification of Americanism with a particular body of economic practices. Some economists have predicted for the future an economic crash similar to that of 1929. If Americanism is equated with competitive capitalism, what happens to it if competitive capitalism comes a cropper? If loyalty and private enterprise are inextricably associated, what is to preserve loyalty if private enterprise fails? Those who associate Americanism with a particular program of economic practices have a grave responsibility, for if their program should fall into disrepute, they expose Americanism itself to disrepute.

The effort to equate loyalty with conformity is misguided because it assumes that there is a fixed content to loyalty and that this can be determined and defined. But loyalty is a principle, and eludes definition except in its own terms. It is devotion to the best interests of the commonwealth, and may require hostility to the particular policies which the government pursues, the particular practices which the economy undertakes, the particular institutions which society maintains. 'If there is any fixed star in our Constitutional constellation,' said the Supreme Court in the Barnette flag-salute case, 'it is that no official, high or petty, can prescribe what shall be orthodox in politics, nationalism, religion, or other matters of opinion, or force citizens to confess by word or act their faith therein. If there are any circumstances which permit an exception they do not now occur to us.'

True loyalty may require, in fact, what appears to the naïve to be disloyalty. It may require hostility to certain provisions of the Constitution itself, and historians have not concluded that those abolitionists who back in the 1840's and 1850's subscribed to the 'Higher Law' were lacking in loyalty. We should not forget that our tradition is one of protest and revolt, and it is stultifying to celebrate the rebels of the past — Jefferson and Paine, Emerson and Thoreau — while we silence the rebels of the present. 'We are a rebellious nation,' said Theodore Parker, known in his day as the Great American Preacher, and went on:

'Our whole history is treason; our blood was attainted before we were born; our creeds are infidelity to the mother church; our constitution, treason to our fatherland. What of that? Though all the governors in the world bid us commit treason against man, and set the example, let us never submit.'

Those who would impose upon us a new concept of loyalty not only assume that this is possible but have the presumption to believe that they are competent to write the definition. We are reminded of Whitman's defiance of the 'never-ending audacity of elected persons.' Who are those who would set the standards of loyalty? They are Rankins and Bilbos, officials of the DAR and the Legion and the NAM, Hearsts and McCormicks. May we not say of Rankin's harangues on loyalty what Emerson said of Webster at the time of his championship of the Fugitive Slave Law of 1850: 'The word honor in the mouth of Mr. Webster is like the word love in the mouth of a whore.'

What do men know of loyalty who make a mockery of the Declaration of Independence and the Bill of Rights, whose energies are dedicated to stirring up race and class hatreds, who would straitjacket the American spirit? What indeed do they know of America — the America of Sam Adams and Tom Paine, of Jackson's defiance of the Court and Lincoln's celebration of labor, of Thoreau's essay on Civil Disobedience and Emerson's championship of John Brown, of the America of the Fourierists and the Come-Outers, of cranks and fanatics, of socialists and anarchists? Who among American heroes could meet their tests, who would be cleared by their committees? Not Washington, who was a rebel. Not Jefferson, who wrote that all men are created equal and whose motto was 'rebellion to tyrants is obedience to God.' Not Garrison, who publicly burned the Constitution; or Wendell Phillips, who spoke for the underprivileged everywhere and counted himself a philosophical anarchist; not Seward of the Higher Law or Sumner of racial equality. Not Lincoln, who admonished us to have malice toward none, charity for all; or Wilson, who warned that our flag was 'a flag of liberty of opinion as well as of political liberty'; or Justice Holmes, who said that our Constitution is an experiment and that while that experiment is being made 'we should be eternally vigilant against attempts to check the expression of opinions that we loathe and believe to be fraught with death.'

* * * *

There are further and more practical objections against the imposition of fixed concepts of loyalty or tests of disloyalty. The effort is itself a confession of fear, a declaration of insolvency. Those who are sure of themselves do not need reassurance, and those who have confidence in the strength and the virtue of America do not need to fear either criticism or competition. The effort is bound to miscarry. It will not apprehend those who are really disloyal, it will not even frighten them; it will affect only those who can be labeled 'radical.' It is sobering to recall that though the Japanese relocation program, carried through at such incalculable cost in misery and tragedy, was justified to us on the ground that the

Japanese were potentially disloyal, the record
does not disclose a single case of Japanese disloyalty or sabotage during the whole war. The
warning sounded by the Supreme Court in the
Barnette flag-salute case is a timely one:

'Ultimate futility of such attempts to compel
obedience is the lesson of every such effort from
the Roman drive to stamp out Christianity as a
disturber of pagan unity, the Inquisition as a
means to religious and dynastic unity, the Si-
berian exiles as a means to Russian unity, down
to the fast-failing efforts of our present totalitarian enemies. Those who begin coercive elimination of dissent soon find themselves extermin-
ating dissenters. Compulsory unification of opinion achieves only the unanimity of the grave-
yard.'

Nor are we left to idle conjecture in this matter; we have had experience enough. Let us limit
ourselves to a single example, one that is wonder-
fully relevant. Back in 1943 the House Un-
American Activities Committee, deeply dis-
turbed by alleged disloyalty among government
employees, wrote a definition of subversive activities and proceeded to apply it. The definition
was admirable, and no one could challenge its
logic or its symmetry:

'Subversive activity derives from conduct intentionally destructive of or inimical to the Government of the United States — that which seeks to undermine its institutions, or to distort its functions, or to impede its projects, or to lessen its efforts, the ultimate end being to overturn it all.'

Surely anyone guilty of activities so defined deserved not only dismissal but punishment. But how was the test applied? It was applied to two scholars, Professors Robert Morss Lovett and Goodwin Watson, and to one young historian, William E. Dodd, Jr., the son of our former Ambassador to Germany. Of almost three million persons employed by the Government, these were the three whose subversive activities were deemed the most pernicious, and the House cut them off the payroll. The sequel is familiar. The Senate concurred only to save a wartime appropriation; the President signed the bill under protest for the same reason. The Supreme Court declared the legislation a 'bill of attainder' and therefore unconstitutional. Who was it, in the end, who engaged in 'subversive activities' — Lovett, Dodd, and Watson, or the Congress which flagrantly violated Article One of the Constitution?

Finally, disloyalty tests are not only futile in application, they are pernicious in their consequences. They distract attention from activities that are really disloyal, and silence criticism inspired by true loyalty. That there are disloyal elements in America will not be denied, but there is no reason to suppose that any of the tests now formulated will ever be applied to them. It is relevant to remember that when Rankin was asked why his Committee did not investigate the Ku Klux Klan he replied that the Klan was not un-American, it was American!

Who are those who are really disloyal? Those who inflame racial hatreds, who sow religious and class dissensions. Those who subvert the Constitution by violating the freedom of the ballot box. Those who make a mockery of majority rule by the use of the filibuster. Those who impair democracy by denying equal educational facilities. Those who frustrate justice by lynch law or by making a farce of jury trials. Those who deny freedom of speech and of the press and of assembly. Those who demand special favors against the interest of the commonwealth. Those who regard public office merely as a source of private gain. Those who would exalt the military over the civil. Those who for selfish and private purposes stir up national antagonisms and expose the world to the ruin of war.

Will the House Committee on Un-American Activities interfere with the activities of these? Will Mr. Truman's disloyalty proclamation reach these? Will the current campaigns for Americanism convert these? If past experience is any guide, they will not. What they will do, if they are successful, is to silence criticism, stamp out dissent — or drive it underground. But if our democracy is to flourish it must have criticism, if our government is to function it must have dissent. Only totalitarian governments insist upon conformity and they — as we know — do so at their peril. Without criticism abuses will go unrebuked; without dissent our dynamic system will become static. The American people have a stake in the maintenance of the most thoroughgoing inquisition into American institutions. They have a stake in nonconformity, for they know that the American genius is nonconformist. They have a stake in experimentation of the most radical character, for they know that only those who prove all things can hold fast that which is good.

It is easier to say what loyalty is not than what it is. It is not conformity. It is not passive acquiescence in the status quo. It is not preference for everything American over everything foreign. It is not an ostrich-like ignorance of other countries and other institutions. It is not the indulgence in ceremony — a flag salute, an oath of allegiance, a fervid verbal declaration. It is not a particular creed, a particular version of history, a particular body of economic practices, a particular philosophy.

It is a tradition, an ideal, and a principle. It is a willingness to subordinate every private advantage for the larger good. It is an appreciation of the rich and diverse contributions that can come from the most varied sources. It is allegiance to the traditions that have guided our greatest statesmen and inspired our most eloquent poets — the traditions of freedom, equality, democracy, tolerance, the tradition of the Higher Law, of experimentation, co-operation, and pluralism. It is a realization that America was born of revolt, flourished on dissent, became great through experimentation.

Independence was an act of revolution; republicanism was something new under the sun; the

federal system was a vast experimental labora-
tory. Physically Americans were pioneers; in the
realm of social and economic institutions, too,
their tradition has been one of pioneering. From
the beginning, intellectual and spiritual diversity
have been as characteristic of America as racial
and linguistic diversity. The most distinctively
American philosophies have been transcendentalism — which is the philosophy of the Higher
Law — and pragmatism — which is the philosophy of experimentation and pluralism. These
two principles are the very core of Americanism:
the principle of the Higher Law, or of obedience
to the dictates of conscience rather than of stat-
utes, and the principle of pragmatism, or the
rejection of a single good and of the notion of
a finished universe. From the beginning Americans have known that there were new worlds to
conquer, new truths to be discovered. Every effort to confine Americanism to a single pattern,
to constrain it to a single formula, is disloyalty
to everything that is valid in Americanism.